The beautiful ceramic and stucco decoration of the portal of the Hlahol choir building at number 248/6 Masarykovo nábřeží

PRAGUE and ART NOUVEAU

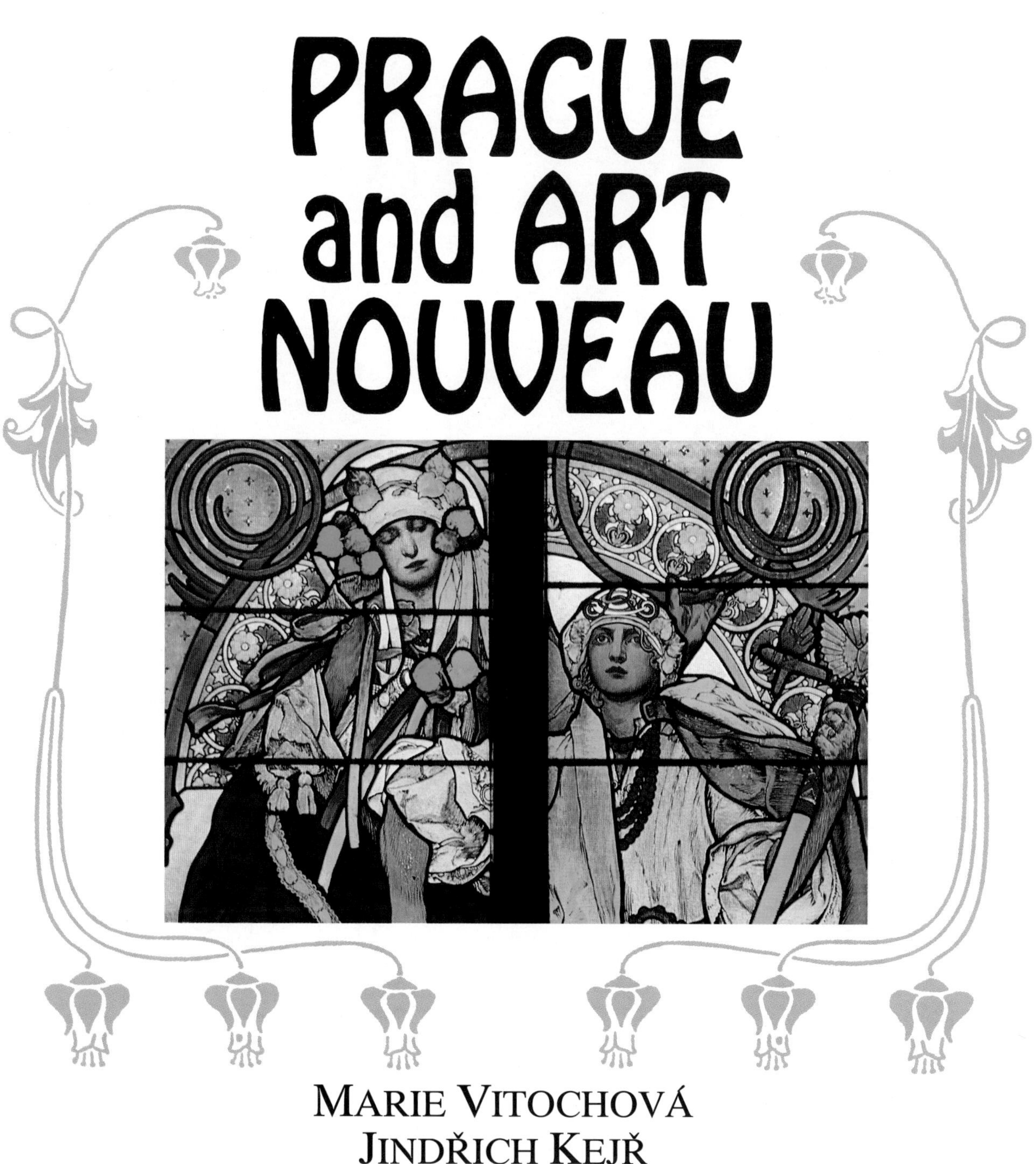

MARIE VITOCHOVÁ
JINDŘICH KEJŘ
JIŘÍ VŠETEČKA

NAKLADATELSTVÍ
V RÁJI

A statue of Wenceslas, patron saint of the Czech lands, and those of two owls, dominate the façade of Art Nouveau house no. 912/6 on Vězeňská Street

ISBN 80-901548-8-3

Every day in Prague one may see visitors and tourists who, map in hand, are eagerly looking for historical monuments and landmarks, craning their necks upwards to the façades of breathtaking Prague houses. Few people are able to provide a knowledgeable answer to the questions posed by these curious lovers of Art Nouveau. With the exception of one very concise brochure, no book dealing with Art Nouveau in Prague which could possibly satisfy the expectations of demanding Art Nouveau enthusiasts, has been available until now.

Considering our everyday contact with visitors to Prague, and our focus on publishing guides to the city, we decided to compile a general educational publication, with the help of which visitors to Prague could go through the streets and acquaint themselves with the places where Art Nouveau has left permanent traces.

What is Art Nouveau Prague? Is it the Municipal House (Obecní dům), the Main Railway Station, or Pařížská Avenue? Is it only the several remarkable buildings that the guides describe? We have intentionally mentioned those places usually recommended to the slightly knowledgeable visitor, or which the visitor already knows. However, this book also aims to take the ordinary visitor to Prague to places he or she would not have reached, or would not have been recommended to see.

After 1900, the rapid development of our expanding capital city was considerably influenced by the Art Nouveau era. Art Nouveau buildings began to supplement, and gradually contribute to the formation of the city's exterior. During the first decade of the 20th century Art Nouveau became a characteristic feature of Czech society, as the Neo-Renaissance had done in the former period. The architecture and sculpture, as well as the painting, of both periods reflected the shifting of the national mentality most prominently: while in the Neo-Renaissance period these aspects manifested themselves more obviously, Art Nouveau did not create big imposing structures, but rather took control of the city in a complex way, dominating whole areas and avenues, thus giving Prague a truly Czech nature as a common fact of life. Art Nouveau succeeded in creating a real environment with its unparallelled style. The Art Nouveau atmosphere of the beginning of century may easily be perceived in the Mayorial Hall of the Municipal House, in Polská Street in Vinohrady, in Kodaňská Street in Vršovice, or for instance in Lesnická Street in Smíchov. That is why we have outlined a series of relaxing walks to help observe the beauties of Art Nouveau and in particular to see the architectonic and sculptural monuments within easy reach of the ordinary sightseer. The walks around the suburbian areas of Prague open up to the visitor an unexpected horizon of views of the Czech capital from places not usually recommended by the travel agencies.

This guide does not aim to be a scientific study of the topic, as this task belongs to the respective institutes and professional scientists. We have drawn upon their theories in studying general signs and themes. A debate as to whether a building is Art Nouveau or not may arise. But even the less knowledgeable visitor will learn that no straight dividing line exists. During the construction of Neo-Renaissance, Neo-Gothic or Neo-Baroque structures, it was often the case that the façade and interior décor were influenced by modern, ornamental, outwardly beautiful but also thematic Art Nouveau elements, or sculptural works and works of art.

So the visitor to Prague may very often see pure Art Nouveau houses or even more frequently houses of older architectonic styles, where inventive, symbolic and relaxed Art Nouveau decoration provided a good breeding ground for architects, or houses with standard Art Nouveau motifs repeated in a strong, rigid manner, somehow even looking austere. This, however, always depended on the builder and his financial situation, or on the special demands or possibilities of the craftsmen to fulfil the task on the basis of a design by a renowned architect. Aside from the well-known buildings which are evidently Art Nouveau in nature, one can also use our guide to find rows of apartment blocks with Art Nouveau façades even in the city districts of Smíchov, Vinohrady, Žižkov, Karlín, Holešovice, Nusle or Vršovice. One will be surprised that in Prague there are actually no two houses that feature the same decoration and thus create uniformity. On the contrary, the master builders and decorators who followed the example of renowned architects such as Osvald Polívka, Jan Kotěra or Bedřich Bendelmayer, developed their own concepts, applying their artistic craftsmanship.

The city of Prague as we proceed through it, begins to show signs of rapid change, mainly manifested in the streets of once suburbian districts. Next to neglected, dirty and worn-out house façades appear newly reconstructed buildings, the colours of their façades shining. It is apparent that these buildings are decorated in the Art Nouveau style. Entering such areas one can imagine how the parts of Prague in

112
NOVÉ MĚSTO
PRAHA
55

which we admired whole "nests" of Art Nouveau houses would look if their exteriors were modified and decorated. But not only their exteriors. Many Prague house interiors have retained their original Art Nouveau and purpose-built elements such as windows, etched or mosaic doors and supraports, mosaic floors, staircase banister grilles and stucco decorations. Many houses feature magnificent products from the RAKO company-fire clay from Rakovník - especially in the mosaic tiles. We might also mention the door grilles, the corner guards, doorplates, and the entire marble tiling in the entrance areas, created with the sensitivity and workmanship of unknown craftsmen.

Having studied sources and collected information, we came across many names of architects, builders, craftsmen, sculptors and painters who made the Prague of the beginning of the 20th century look like a modern and breathtaking city only with their skill and hard work learned from their stays and studies in France, Austria and Germany, from where they also drew their inspiration and, moreover, the determination to bring something new to Prague, thus enhancing the image of a bustling western city. The reader will gradually become familiar with their names as well.

The book contains fifteen chapters, each of which represents one separate short or longer walk through Prague. It is formulated in such a way that the visitor, using public transport with little difficulty and carrying nothing more than a simple map, will be capable of completing the walk. The visitor will be able to breathe the unique modern atmosphere of ordinary city districts, visit cheaper shops and pubs and meet ordinary Prague citizens. Prague offers so many Art Nouveau memories that this book could not possibly attempt to give an exhaustive view of the subject. We may, however, state that after taking the walks this book recommends, the visitor will have obtained a sufficient picture of what Prague can offer in terms of Art Nouveau architecture.

The book was commenced in the summer of 1993, and owing to the shortage of time, the wealth of sources in this field and the study required, it could not have been finished in such a short time were it not for the understanding and peaceful atmosphere our families provided for us. Neither should we forget our loyal and very helpful colleague, Jiří Všetečka, who with patience and enthusiasm took photographs in often impenetrable city traffic simply to meet our demanding requirements. We met many people who were interested in this field while collecting information and observing the buildings on the spot. Most of them displayed great interest in our work, gave us help and advice, and especially ordinary citizens from the so-called unattractive areas of Prague expressed true delight over such a contribution to opening up Prague. Special thanks should go to the management of hotels Evropa, Paříž and Union, Villa Voyta, The Municipal House and The National House in Smíchov, to Chief Physician Jaroslava Lukešová from Kojenecký ústav v Krči (Children's Institute in Krč) and to Mr. Starý, teacher of arts and crafts at Karlín school.

Last but not least, we should like to express our gratitude to the team led by Mr. Jaroslav Skřivan and Mr. Petr Mareš of the printing house in Pardubice.

MARIE VITOCHOVÁ
JINDŘICH KEJŘ

TRANSLATOR'S NOTE

The majority of street names used in the book have been left in Czech without translation. The following guide may help the reader to decipher their meaning at least partially, and should be used when asking for directions in Prague.

budova - building
dům - house
nábřeží - embankment
náměstí - square
třída - avenue
ulice - street

DENIS RATH
MARK PRESCOTT

The portal of a building on Spálená Street, considered to be an Art Nouveau paraphrase of the Baroque in the work of Osvald Polívka

1 WALKS THROUGH ART NOUVEAU PRAGUE

The portal of the so-called Peterka House at number 777/12 Wenceslas Square, the central feature of which is the Madonna and Child. The Virgin Mary is clothed in a simple gilded dress

Wenceslas Square is the centre of a modern city, especially sought after nowadays for its dense network and wide range of shops and department stores, travel agencies, banks and transport network (two of the most important railway junctions - the Main Station and Masaryk. Station - are locuted close by). Unfortunately, however, a main road now separates the square from the National Museum. Wenceslas Square became more important in the second half of the nineteenth century, when the political and commercial centre of Prague finally moved here from the Old Town Square. The metropolitan character of the square - a modern boulevard - culminated in the construction of new palaces and houses along both sides of the extensive square, which is 683 metres long and 60 metres wide. The large-scale construction of new houses, palaces and shops in the second half of the 19th century reflects almost all styles employed from approximately 1860 until now. Fortunately enough, the square has been spared the construction of the tasteless prefabricated buildings and ugly monuments of recent times.

After the foundation of Prague New Town in 1348, the site of the present square served as a large market, mainly trading in horses, and thus the place acquired the name the Horse Market, which was used until 1848. Since completion of the first stage of city construction at the close of the 19th century, the whole square has been dominated by the immense Neo-Renaissance building of the National Museum, with its façade facing Wenceslas Square. It stands on a site occupied until the demolition of city walls by the Horse Gate - one of the main medieval gates. At the top part of the square, below the museum, is a place of strong emotive and political significance in the modern history of the nation: the equestrian statue of St. Wenceslas by Josef Václav Myslbek, with four patron saints of Bohemia guarding the corners of the pedestal, is both a symbol and a legend.

As a result of the period in which historicizing styles dominated architecture, in Prague it is especially the Neo-Renaissance and Neo-Gothic which are so impressively displayed on Wenceslas Square (the Neo-Renaissance building of the National Museum, Wiehl House at no. 792, or the Neo-Baroque palace Assicurazioni Generali dating from the end of the 19th century, by achitects Bedřich Ohmann and Osvald Polívka at the corner of Wenceslas Square and Jindřišská Street are examples). The subsequent rise of architectonic Art Nouveau (known here as "secese") found its place in the area, both in the composition of buildings and in their decoration.

The pretty Art Nouveau ornamentation on this façade at no. 761/1 Jungmannovo Square is an example of the Art Nouveau stucco technique employing vegetal motifs

One of the first Art Nouveau houses still standing today, the so-called Peterka House at no. 777/12 dating from 1899, is situated in the lower part of Wenceslas Square. It is also one of the first houses built by the renowned architect Jan Kotěra. The house, built in the style of the early Art Nouveau, has a typical three-axial composition with a high plinth on the ground floor designed for commercial activities. The striking simplicity of the façade for that period and the efficiently conceived, unusual design of the interior of the building, expressed the hierarchy of the individual components in the creation of architectural work as stated by Kotěra: function, design and form. The floors of the house have a slightly arched central part and the thinner lateral axes are completed with triple gables. The balance of purpose and decoration was reflected in the size of the windows and in the ratio of the plain surface to the ornamentation of the façade. The impression of characteristic verticality was created not only by a high stone plinth on the ground floor which opened through a passage to the yard, lined by ashlar pilasters and decorated with a Madonna dressed in gold carrying the Christ Child, but also by the gradual segmentation of the upper floors. The central part of the house is dominated by sculptures by Stanislav Sucharda, placed alongside a balcony on the uppermost floor. The central part of the house also displays a richer, typical floral decoration in stucco, and the colours of the stucco decoration are in harmony with that of the plain surface of the façade. Fine stucco foliage decorates the upper corners of the window openings on the lateral axes of the house, and is also repeated inside on the ornamental floral decoration and the mosaic tiling of the corridors and on the

The frontispieces of interesting buildings on Wenceslas Square. Moving from left to right we see Peterka House, an Art Nouveau structure by Jan Kotěra dating from 1899; the Neo-Baroque-style Art Nouveau building at no. 776/10, called U Trojice, by architect Alois Dlabač with sculptures by Ladislav Šaloun, František Rous and Vilém Amort; and the building called U Zlatého Noha at no. 775/8, designed by architect Matěj Blecha and dating from 1912-1913

staircase grating, as well as on the decorative but practical handrails that protect the corners of the corridors. By way of interest, a small yard offers the visitor an unusual glimpse of the tall apse of the presbytery of the Gothic Church of Our Lady of the Snows (chrám Panny Marie Sněžné).

The decoration of Peterka House is severe and sober in colour, in the Art Nouveau style which is typical of Prague and is the work of Josef Pekárek and Stanislav Sucharda. Peterka House was the very first to be built by Kotěra after his arrival from Vienna. Even then, as he began his creative architectonic work, Kotěra demonstrated his penchant for austerity in designing functional buildings and his inclination towards later styles of the modern movement. But the most outstanding, as well as the largest Art Nouveau building on Wenceslas Square, is the Evropa Hotel.

The publicity slogan "U Šroubků (At the Šroubeks') in life - in heaven after death" was borrowed from a booklet written and published by Karel Šroubek, the owner of the Grand Hotel on Wenceslas Square, in 1938. The Grand Hotel Šroubek, formerly "Archduke Stephen Hotel" is nowadays called the

The lower part of Wenceslas Square. Towering above an else in this shot is the tower of the Koruna Palace. An Art Nouveau palace is located at no. 377/13 28. října Street, to the left of the smaller, late Baroque building known as Úl (The Hive)

Evropa Hotel and represents a significant accomplishment of Prague Art Nouveau architecture.

The Archduke Stephen hotel building, constructed in 1889 by the architect Quidon Bělský for the then owner, Vilém Hauner, had to be rebuilt fairly soon to meet the requirements of the new age and the modern way of life coming into existence at the turn of the century. The reconstruction was carried out in 1903-1904 by Bedřich Bendelmayer and Alois Dryák, important architects of the time in Art Nouveau style. Although the façade of the building is, unlike other Art Nouveau structures of that kind, fairly extensively (two-dimensionally) decorated, it creates a strong and grand impression, thanks to the variety of detail, the colours and the use of gilding, as well as the originality of the forged grating of the balconies. The visitor will be particularly attracted by the front gable of the main building, which bears a gilded sign and a coloured glass mosaic, created on a design by the painter Jan Förster. It does not lack a typical element of Art Nouveau façades - a vegetable wreath with rib-

The Grand Hotel Evropa on Wenceslas Square, with its elaborately decorated façade culminating in a coat of arms. The allegorical sculptural group on the coat of arms is the work of the well-known Czech sculptor, Ladislav Šaloun

bons between the windows, accentuated by glazed coloured tiles. Similar stylized floral decorations may be found especially on the top floor of the adjoining, thinner hotel section, which culminates, moreover, in an impressive forged banister with a period eye-catcher. The space above the façade gable is dominated by a group of sculptures - fairies surrounding a lantern - a work of the famous academic sculptor Ladislav Šaloun.

A balcony with an imaginative grating stretches alongside the level of the mezzanin café. The entrance is protected by a glazed marquise, typical of the Art Nouveau style.

The beautiful interior was designed jointly by the architects Bohumil Hypšman and Jan Letzel, and the café built by Jindřich Röhrs on a design by the architect Richard Hirschl. The mural paintings were created by the painter Láďa Novák. The overall appearance and functionality of the interior is a result of the work and creations of a number of predominantly Czech firms of craftsmen: the decorative railings were supplied

Glorious Art Nouveau decoration, comprising floral and spiral elements, on the awning which covers the main entrance to the Grand Hotel Evropa

A detail of the extraordinary décor inside the French restaurant at the Grand Hotel Evropa (formerly Hotel Šroubek): a bronze lamp standing beside a mirror

This shot of the interior of the French restaurant at the Grand Hotel Evropa on Wenceslas Square is enough to tempt anyone to visit it

Wenceslas Square and the Grand Hotel Evropa as seen at night.
The dominant feature on the square, however, is the
Neo-Renaissance National Museum

the firm of Faltus and Koutník, the light fittings by Franta Anýž, and the firm of Suda and Kotěšovec, the central heating by the firm of Jan Štětka, the electricity distribution by the Kolben & Company factory, and the electric lifts were installed by a Viennese firm Wertheim & Company

Consistent with the European standards of the time, the hotel was divided into a French restaurant, café and bar. It has a Mirrored Hall and a Pilsen restaurant. At that time, the hotel succeeded in providing its guests with top comfort and luxury both in its restaurants and in the hotel section, which had a capacity of approximately two hundred beds in ninety rooms and suites. "Šroubek's" cuisine soon made the hotel famous and attracted even those who, during their visit to Prague, were not lucky enough to obtain accommodation in the hotel.

It was the new proprietor (1924), Karel Šroubek, and his wife Viléma, who brought the hotel its renown and gathered inside the hotel a whole collection of works of art, including superb Ming vases and precious paintings. In keeping with their motto: "What satisfies our guest satisfies us," the Šroubeks created a comfortable, exclusive and decent atmosphere and attracted a number of well-known figures of national and international political life who made the hotel their favourite. To mention just a few, the hotel register contains the names of the Czech-born mayor of Chicago (Mr. Čermák), of Czechoslovak government officials Beran, Msgr. Šrámek, Krofta and Hodža, and of other eminent personalities; only recently, in 1989, Shirley Temple-Black stayed in the hotel.

The hotel has been preserved in its original state, which includes beautiful inlaid wooden panelling, chandeliers and Art Nouveau ornamentation in the corridors and lounges. The hotel offers its guests a surprisingly peaceful and cosy atmosphere, though the building is situated in the very centre of the metropolitan hustle and bustle and within reach of big department stores, banks, the underground and other transport systems. The Evropa Hotel has succesfully taken up the tradition of the Grand Hotel Šroubek. The building still retains the atmosphere created by the harmony of functionality and art, another of the main objectives of Art Nouveau artists.

Before leaving Wenceslas Square, you will certainly notice other interesting buildings. Directly opposite the Evropa Hotel, viewed from the café gallery, we see a huge building called Lucerna (The Lantern), built by the architect Václav Havel in 1913-1917 as the first ferroconcrete building in Prague. The adjoining house, with a lavishly decorated façade, was built in 1911-1912 on a design by the architect Bedřich Bendelmayer. The view on the opposite side ends with a house built by a renowned architect of the Czech Neo-Renaissance, Antonín Wiehl. The façade of the house is decorated by outstanding murals based upon sketches by Mikoláš Aleš

A typical feature on Art Nouveau buildings: a sculptured mascaron on the building at no. 761/1 Jungmannovo Square

and Josef Fanta. If we walk along the lower part of the square, we cannot fail to notice the buildings of Zlatá Husa (The Golden Goose) Hotel at no. 839 (built in 1910 by the firm of Matěj Blecha, the architect of the façade being Emil Králíček) and the Ambassador Hotel at no. 840 (built by the proprietor and designer František Weyr). The architect Richard Klenka and the architect and builder Josef Jánský participated in the design of the Ambassador. The proprietor of the new building, situated on the site of the former house known as "U Zlatého beránka" (The Golden Lamb), gave Klenka an opportunity to realize his ideas and he then designed the frontal in the style of the new wave of Art Nouveau ornamentism. Since its reconstruction in 1919-1923 the Ambassador has served as a hotel. Unfortunately, the classicising Art Nouveau construction has been adapted several times, not always successfully, and the original Art Nouveau decorations of the exterior and interior have been partially removed. The largest palace in the lower part of the square, erected in the style of modern movement, is called Koruna (The Crown) with its characteristic corner tower. It was built in 1911-1914, and its sculptural decoration was made by Stanislav Sucharda and Jan Štursa. The architect was Antonín Pfeiffer.

From Wenceslas Square we continue our walk around the city centre by turning to the left into 28. října street. If we look up, we can admire the Baroque classicist house on the right, standing at the very beginning of the street. The house is called "Úl" (The Hive), according to the sculpture on the front gable. But we should especially notice the early Art Nouveau house at no. 377/13, designed by the architect Osvald Polívka, constructed in 1902 by the builder Matěj Blecha and decorated by Celda Klouček. The house is topped by a huge allegorical figural group in the attic, supplemented by vegetal growth and vases on the banister, which are then symbolically repeated above the entrances to the house. In the centre, below the main cornice, is a sign "Built in A. D. 1902". Although the stucco decoration of the façade synthetizes the Neo-Baroque and Art Nouveau elements, the richness of stylised floral designs, allegorical mascarons and vases, accentuated by Art Nouveau letters and ribbon ornamentation, indicates the dominance of Art Nouveau decoration. The front of the house is made of sandstone and produces a rough impression, but a marble combination is used on the walls in the interior, and the foyer contains metallic alloys and glass, which are also used on the interesting wall lanterns and the functional glass ceiling. This is of great importance in a building which usually houses exhibitions of works of art and non-decorative objects. The plaster decoration of the interior is the work of Karel Novák.

As we walk along the street, we pass other noteworthy buildings such as no. 376/11, "U Tří bílých beránků" (The Three White Lambs), built in 1895 by the architect Bedřich Ohmann, and no. 375/9, built to the design of the architect Eduard Sochor. The houses are built in historicising styles, with fine façades and outstandingly intricate balcony grilles.

The corner of 28. října Street and Jungmannovo Square is dominated by a huge, grand building called the Department Store (Obchodní dům), which has a genuinely Art Nouveau decorated entrance from Jungmannovo Square. The house was built in 1906 by Josef Kandert, probably according to a design by Karel Mottl.

The house stands on the corner and symmetrically diverges into two streets; its sides bear outstanding round bays topped with round towers, gables and vast plant decoration with big vases. The gable which sits atop the main, wide façade is the largest, and behind it rises a stylised cupola with ornaments. The surface of the gable is broken by a large window opening surrounded by a vast plastic wreath of stucco foliage and fruit. The house is horizontally segmented by bands and parapet ledges; the stucco decoration under the balconies and bays, especially on the first floor, seems to be multiplied into several layers and produces an impressive sculptural effect of abstract foliage and cones. The balcony grille, shaped in the form of flowers, is very impressive, as is the large mascaron situated under the balcony on the main frontal. The Department Store is noteworthy for its new, different conception of the mascaron and unusually lavish plaster decoration, which gives the onloocker an insight into the Art Nouveau technique of plaster application.

We now turn back to Jungmannovo Square, which is dominated by a monument of the Czech "awakener", Josef Jungmann, pass a famous restaurant "U Pinkasů" and return through a passageway to Wenceslas Square. Here, to the right of the Bata department store, by the house no. 775/8 called "U Zlatého noha" (The Golden Griffin, formerly Adam's Pharmacy) we complete our first Prague Art Nouveau walk. The building is functional and severe, dating from the post-Art Nouveau period, its surface decoration created by the combination of non-plaster brickwork and smooth plastering, and has a sober plaster decoration. It was built by the firm of Matěj Blecha. The notable severity of the house is accentuated in comparison with the adjoining house no. 776/10, "U Trojice" (Trinity). The house was built in 1899 by the architect Alois Dlabač, and is adorned with large sculptures by Ladislav Šaloun, František Rous and Vilém Amort.

An Art Nouveau palace at no. 377/13 28. října Street, erected in 1902 by Matěj Blecha on a design by Osvald Polívka. The decoration on the façade is by Celda Klouček; the sculptural adornments in the interior are the work of Karel Novák

2 WALKS THROUGH ART NOUVEAU PRAGUE

This detail from a stained-glass window, the late Art Nouveau work of Alfons Mucha, depicts a scene from the lives of SS Cyril and Methodius

The most exquisite Prague monument, St. Vitus' Cathedral, is also a good place to start a walk to uncover the beauties of the architecture, sculpture and painting of the Prague Art Nouveau. The whole extensive complex of Prague Castle involves splendid works of art in almost all architectural styles. But it is only in St. Vitus' Cathedral that we may find works by Art Nouveau artists. The cathedral was completed between 1893 and 1929, and although it was adapted in austere, almost purifying Neo-Gothic style, during the period in which the construction was overseen by Kamil Hilbert modern architectonic ideas also found their place.

The decoration was significantly influenced by the painters and sculptors of the period, many of whom ranked among the prominent artists of the Bohemian Art Nouveau, and this was clearly reflected in their work. For example,

Bílek's sculptural group entitled "Komenský se loučí s vlastí" (Comenius departs from his native land) stands in front of his original villa at the corner of Mickiewiczova Street in Hradčany

A stained-glass window by Alfons Mucha in the Archbishop's Chapel of St. Vitus' Cathedral

The colourful evening sky over
St. Vitus' Cathedral at
Prague Castle

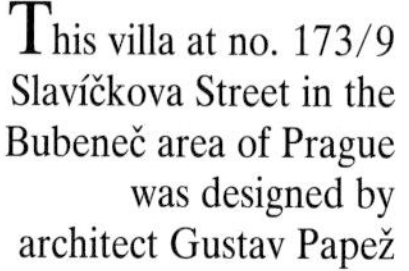

This villa at no. 173/9 Slavíčkova Street in the Bubeneč area of Prague was designed by architect Gustav Papež

after completion of the façade, the cathedral contained fourteen sculptures of saints and a sculpture of Charles IV, by the sculptors Čeněk Vosmík, Stanislav Sucharda and others whose names had by that time already been linked with significant, genuinely Art Nouveau buildings in Prague.

In St. Vitus's Cathedral we can certainly admire windows made to designs by prominent Czech painters and artists such as Max Švabinský, František Kysela and Alfons Mucha. The latter's work, described as late Art Nouveau, was given as a gift by a former insurance company Slavie. The stained-glass window, dating from 1931, pictures a scene from the life of the saints Cyril and Methodius. Mucha's window differs in style from the other windowpanes, and cannot conceal the work of this Slavic epic. A generous colour conception, in which the yellow and red centre fades into lighter colours at the edges, is typical of Mucha's treatment of colours.

In addition to the famous window, the visitor will certainly stop to gaze in admiration at the windows designed by other artists, most of which were installed in the 1930s and designed by Max Švabinský, František Kysela, Cyril Bouda and

Part of the painted façade with floral motifs of the Papež villa on Slavíčkova Street

An Art Nouveau villa at no. 196/7 Slavíčkova Street. The building was designed by architect Karel Vítězslav Mašek; the sculpture of the Madonna and Child is the work of sculptor Ludvík Wurzel

Karel Svolinský. The work of Max Švabinský, a master of figural drawing who was prolific during the Art Nouveau period, is especially remarkable. Švabinský is also the author of the largest number of models for the windows installed in the 1930s. Chief amongst them is a stained-glass window in the Chapel of St. Ludmila (Kaple sv. Ludmily), created on to one of his designs. The window illustrates the Descent of the Holy Spirit.

Walking around the cathedral, one also notices the large carved Crucifixion by František Bílek, dating from 1899, in the aisle to the left behind the new sacristy. Bílek is also the author of the stone memorial to those who died in the First World War, which stands in the corner of St. Wenceslas' Chapel. Here also stands a marble figure of Christ by Čeněk Vosmík, dated 1912. The tour around the Castle should be rounded off with a visit to the picture galleries in the Sternberk Palace (Šternberský palác) and the Riding School of Prague Castle (Jízdárna Pražského hradu). After that we should take a stroll around the Royal Garden (Královská zahrada) towards the Royal Summer Palace (Královský letohrádek). From here the Chotek Gardens (Chotkovy sady) are within easy reach.

In this vast landscape composition one cannot fail to see an artificial rock. This allegorical group of white marble is a surprising feature of the rock's recess-grotto. The visitor has just reached the memorial to the poet Julius Zeyer. The sculptures in the cave under a portrait plaque of Zeyer impersonate allegorically significant figures in the poet's works. A stylistically late work by Josef Mauder dating from 1913 thus reminds us that Art Nouveau also had a sentimentally romantic impact.

Immediately at the crossroads of the Chotek Gardens and Mickiewicz Street, surrounded by a garden, stands the studio house of a significant representative of symbolism and Art Nouveau, the sculptor František Bílek. Villa no. 233/1, built in 1911, expresses the sculptor's life-long effort to find an ideological anchor for his work, which had its basis in religion and its literary sources, especially the Bible. In the construction of his villa, Bílek was inspired by the idea of a cornfield, which he expressed by immense columns in the style of ancient Egypt. It was also the first structure conceived with a flat roof. The villa as a whole is a unique work of art, which gives the impression of a single symbolic, spiritually percepted sculpture made up of segmented material on the rough walls, sculpturally formed concrete columns and the massive horizontal of the flat roof. In the garden in front of the villa is Bílek's sculptural group from 1926 entitled "Comenius departs from his native land".

The adjoining villa, no. 234/3, was built between 1910 and 1911 by Antonín Hulán and was probably designed by Ladislav Procházka. In 1912 František Bílek decorated it with his reliefs. The ornamental character of the flat façade is achieved by the combination of smooth and rough plastering and by plaster ornaments on the ledges around the windows. In the corner bay is an interesting stone lantern. Walking further along the street we reach houses no. 240/15 and

A detail from the exterior of the Hanava Pavilion.Use of new materials was made in the design and construction of the exterior

The coat of arms on the frontal of the Hanava Pavilion, an attractive Neo-Baroque structure erected for the National Jubilee Exhibition in 1891

no. 239/13, designed by the architect Jan Kotěra between 1910 and 1911. A bust of Charlotte Masaryk by Vojtěch Sucharda is located on house no. 239/13. Attention should be also paid to house no. 254/6 on the opposite side, which bears a relief of Jan Hus and a sign "With the sword of truth you broke the bonds of phantoms". If we walk along the street called Na Baště svaté Ludmily, we will get a clear picture of the remarkable houses from the period between 1910 and 1920. Among the most interesting is house no. 247/13, built in 1913 by the architect Emil Králíček. This part of the Hradčany, as a whole, is one of the most successful urban constructions of modern Prague.

A roughly ten-minute walk will lead us from the Bílek Villa to the left along Badeniho Street, across the junction with Milady Horákové Avenue to Majakovského Street, and by turning to the left we reach a quiet street, Na Zátorce, in the district of Bubeneč. We should note that on the corner with the street Pod Kaštany stands the 1916 memorial to the composer Karel Bendl by Stanislav Sucharda. Among the houses of the street stand out no. 289/3 (architects Matěj Blecha and Emil Králíček) and no. 350/5, built by Antonín Pfeiffer in 1912.

If we walk further along we reach Suchardova Street, where we should pay attention to villa no. 284/4, and especially to its stately vaulted entrance and decoration with prominent colourful tiles. The house was built in 1905 by the architect Dušan Jurkovič, and represents a kind of a Nordic building. Opposite the house is villa no. 248/8, designed in 1904 by Jan Kotěra for Stanislav Sucharda. It is a large villa with an adjoining studio built for Sucharda's work on the memorial to František Palacký. In addition to the building itself, Kotěra's design also included an intimate functional urban garden.

Directly opposite, in Slavíčkova Street, we can see Art Nouveau villa no. 196/7. Mašek Villa is by the architect Karel Vítězslav Mašek and has a notable corner relief of the Madonna and Child by the sculptor Ludvík Wurzel. The façade is decorated (by the sculptor Antonín Waigant) with painted plaster floral ornaments. The neighbouring house, no. 173/9, was built in around 1899 by the builder Gustav Papež in genuinely Art Nouveau style. The decoration on the façade is restricted to abstract floral motifs. Besides Art Nouveau villas, the street also includes Neo-Renaissance houses, noteworthy both for their decoration and the importance of their former occupants. Several tens of metres onwards we can admire a pre-Art Nouveau house at no. 151/15, built between 1895 and 1896 by the architect Jan Koula as a Neo-Renaissance buiding with frescoes. On the front of the house is the fresco "Božetěch, abbot of Sázava", based on a sketch by Mikoláš Aleš and created by Arnošt Hofbauer. The sign on the gable reminds us for whom the villa was originally designed: "Erected and paid for by the sculptor Sucharda and his wife Anna in 1895". Under the main ledge, in sculptured floral plaster we can see gables which remind us of the names of prominent Czech artists. Next to the building the architect Jan Koula built his own villa, no. 153/17, in 1896, in folk style.

We leave Slavíčkova Street by returning to Majakovského and Badeniho and opposite the Bílek Villa will left into street Bašta svatého Tomáše (St. Thomas' Bastion). Here we can find architectonically interesting houses no. 232/3 by the architect Alois Čenský (dating from 1911 and adapted by Kamil Hilbert in 1924) and no. 231/5 by Rudolf Stockar (built between 1910 and 1911). A pleasant Art Nouveau villa may be found at no. 228/8. House no. 228/8 was built in 1911 by the architect František Schlaffer. Its façade has a balcony decorated with relief bowls containing flowers and fruit and distinctive decoration on the ledges around the windows. The corner bay is protected by a roof on columns. A little further towards the end of Gogol Street stands Neo-Baroque villa no. 212/1, designed by the architect Bedřich Ohmann from 1908-1911 and villa no. 225/2 (from 1911) by the architect Alois Čenský.

From here we head through the Letná Gardens (Letenské sady) to the Hanava Pavilion (Hanavský pavilon). Hanava Pavilion offers a spectacular view of Prague. It is sometimes mistakenly described as a Art Nouveau work - maybe because the construction already employed modern materials such as iron and glass, and even some decorative Art Nouveau elements. The Pavilion was moved to its present location in 1898 from the complex of the 1891 Jubilee Exhibition. It is a Neo-Baroque structure cast in iron at the Komárov Foundries, on a design by the architect Heiser. Its plaster decoration was designed by the architect Josef Herdík and implemented by Zdeněk Emanuel Fiala. The Pavilion was presented to the city by William, Prince of Hanava. Since expensive reconstruction work between 1966 and 1968 the building serves as a café and restaurant.

The Pavilion is very impressive when viewed from the Vltava embankment, especially from the Art Nouveau Svatopluka Čecha Bridge.

3 WALKS THROUGH ART NOUVEAU PRAGUE

A mascaron of an aged human face above an arched window under the oriel of the house called the Red Anchor at no. 1527/9 Na Švihance Street

Today's walk will explore Prague Art Nouveau beauties in two old suburbs of Prague. Vinohrady and neighbouring Žižkov grew in the course of the 19th century beyond the city walls, and at first were independent of the rest of the city. The best way to reach them is to take underground on the A line train at Můstek (Little Bridge) Station, at the bottom of Wenceslas Square, and alight at the second station - Náměstí Míru (Peace Square), our destination. We emerge beside the Church of St. Ludmila (kostel sv. Ludmily), that dominates the whole square, and the place where we begin our walk. We now find ourselves in the district of Vinohrady.

The Vineyard Hills (Hory Viničné) were renamed Vinohrady in 1849 and in 1867 Královské Vinohrady (the Royal Vineyards). In 1875 they split into the municipalities of Žižkov and Královské Vinohrady, and finally, in 1879,

Královské Vinohrady area was granted the status of a town. Until the formation of Greater Prague in 1922, the town rejected all attempts to merge with historical Prague. Until the second half of the nineteenth century there were sparse homesteads, alleys and gardens, the names of which are still contained in streets and buildings.

But in the second half of the 19th century this area, just as any other suburbian district of Prague, saw the beginnings of economic prosperity. Especially at the end of the 19th century Vinohrady had been developing at a breathtaking pace, due to the enterpreneurial and economic rise of the Czech bourgeoisie and the wealth of the administration officials who had settled here in large numbers. The urban build-up also expanded rapidly, the number of inhabitants increased and all this resulted in the need to build social, commercial and cultural centres for the town. It was at that time that the central Vinohrady square (náměstí Míru) began to acquire its architectural character. The most significant buildings for civic and social purposes - the Church of St. Ludmila, the National House (Národní dům) and the theatre, were concentrated on the square.

As a result of the construction of the first railway line, the northern part of Vinohrady was busy with construction activities, which were allowed to flourish until 1870. At that time, during the construction of a gasworks, the local mayor and builder, Karel Hartig, drafted a firm regulatory plan for other building activity. Hartig also gave the district its new name: in 1887 it was christened Žižkov, in memory of the famous hussite military leader, who in 1420 fought a victorious battle on Vítkov Hill with the crusading armies. In 1881 Žižkov was also given the

The frontispiece of Vinohrady Theatre (Vinohradské divadlo) is elaborately decorated with many different Art Nouveau mascarons and sculptures. The herms were created by Bohumil Kafka

Vinohrady Theatre: a magnificent Art Nouveau structure by the architect Alois Čenský dating from 1904-1907. Behind it, standing on a street corner, is a Neo-Baroque building boasting a richly decorated façade

status of a town (in 1922 it became a part of Greater Prague).

The ground plan of Žižkov is made up of three avenues diverging from the end of Hybernská Street: Husitská Street stretches under the hill-side of Vítkov, Seifertova Avenue runs upwardly into Táboritská, and the third street, U Rajské zahrady, runs towards Vinohradská Avenue.

Our walk only enters Žižkov only briefly, since the houses with Art Nouveau façades are situated mainly in the part which closely adjoins Vinohrady, but we should at least mention some significant places which are worth seeing.

Vítkov Hill represents a clearly visible dominant of Žižkov and of the whole Prague lying to the east of the centre. On the hill stands a monument and an ostentatious bronze equestrian statue of Jan Žižka by Bohumil Kafka, who was, at a certain stage of his work, influenced by the fashionable Art Nouveau. Kafka's equestrian statue has been standing on a huge pedestal on Vítkov Hill since 1950. It was made by the well-known firm of the metal founder Václav Mašek, on a design by Bohumil Kafka.

An important pseudo-Gothic monument is the parish church of St. Procopius on Sladkovského Square, which adjoins the upper part of Seifertova Avenue. It was built as a three-nave column hall with a front tower between 1899 and 1903, and was designed by the architects Josef Mocker and František Mikš. The tympanon of the main portal bears a relief by Josef Pekárek, and a remarkable painting of St. Wenceslas by Karel Škréta, painted in as early as 1649, should be noted in the interior.

A stunning ceramic biblical scene in the Neo-Gothic Church of St. Ludmila on náměstí Míru (Peace Square) in Vinohrady

A Gothic-style Art Nouveau altar consecrated to Our Lady and the Czech patron saints in the Church of St. Ludmila in Vinohrady

House no. 1557/8 on the corner of Čerchovská and Krkonošská Streets, dates from 1911. The large symbolic architectonic structure represents Krakonoš, ruler of the nation's mountains

Havlíčkovo Square contains buildings of the former Žižkov Town Hall, built around 1890 in the style of the Neo-Renaissance by the architect Jan Šimáček.

An important place in the Žižkov area is the former Jewish cemetery in Fibichova Street. The cemetery is situated directly below the television transmitter, an ugly dominant feature of Prague. It came into existence during the plague of 1680, when a lazaret for the Jewish inhabitants of Prague was erected on the site. The cemetery was still used during the plague of 1715, and again from 1787 until the second half of the last century.

Both towns - Žižkov and Vinohrady - expanded, and their construction progressed simultaneously; however, buildings in each of them had their special features. While uncomfortable blocks of flats were constructed in Žižkov, their small flats occupied by relatively poor people, the more wealthy burghers of Vinohrady naturally constructed more spacious buildings, with more demanding requirements for comfort. The wider possibilities of Vinohrady are reflected in civic buidings, and in larger and more ostentatious houses that those in Žižkov. One of them - an insurance company building at Londýnská no. 136/54 - was designed in 1912 by the experienced architect Osvald Polívka.

Unfortunately, the only part of the interior which was preserved by the famous insurance company is a hall with picturesque decoration.

After a brief introduction to the history of Vinohrady and Žižkov, we can finally start our walk. We are standing at the metro exit by the church. The Church of St. Ludmila is a Neo-Gothic brick basilic, with two front towers and a transept, built in the North German Gothic style between 1888 and 1893, to the design by Josef Mocker. The likeness of St. Ludmila in the relief above the main portal was created by the sculptor Josef Václav Myslbek.

Of particular note are two later side altars in Gothic-Art Nouveau style. They were carved according to drawings by Jan Kastner and Štěpán Zálešák, and also employ Art Nouveau vegetal ornamentation. The left altar is consecrated to the Virgin Mary and the Bohemian patron saints, and the right altar to SS Cyril and Methodius. Both altars illustrate how Art Nouveau decoration found its place in sacred art. In the centre of the church, both sides of the aisles are lined with plaster reliefs depicting biblical scenes.

Behind the church, between Slezská and Korunní Streets, stands the National House (Národní dům) at no. 820, a two-winged Neo-Renaissance structure dating from 1893-1894. The statues and busts on the façade are the work of Antonín Popp.

Also behind the Church of St. Ludmila rises the remarkable building of the Vinohrady Theatre (Divadlo na Vinohradech), built in Art Nouveau style. It has great significance as a unifying element of the square, as it shifts the orientation from the Church of St. Ludmila to the northern side of the square through its rigidly symmetrical material composition, crowned with two towers.

At the beginning of the 20th century the municipal council invited tenders from Bohemian architects for a design for the Vinohrady Theatre. The first prize was awarded to the architect Alois Čenský, the second prize to the architect Antonín Balšánek.

After some adaptations to Alois Čenský's designs, construction commenced in 1904 and it was only on the 24 November 1907 that gave its an opening performance. Contemporary sources claim that the construction cost 800 000 crowns. In the design of the building, its author, Alois Čenský, followed the Art Nouveau taste of the period, although the work as a whole cannot conceal the architect's developing a new form from a firm basis of well-tried principles of historical composition. A marquise protrudes above a three-door entrance from a huge central risalit on the front facing the square, and is supported by spiral buttresses lavishly decorated with foliage. The marquise also has hanging lights. The whole front of the building is crowned with a pair of pylons with the symbolic groups of the "Truth" and "Courage" created by the sculptor Milan Havlíček in 1906. The main cornice bears outstanding herms by the sculptor Bohumil Kafka. The main entrances lead into the foyer, decorated by Antonín Popp. From here there are entrances to the galleries around the whole auditorium of the theatre. Stairs to the balconies are located both on the right and on the left. Above the foyer is a large lounge. The sculptural decoration of the proscenium and boxes is the work of Antonín Mára and the painting on the ceiling of the auditorium entitled "Homage to the Art of the Country" was created by František Urban. The curtain, dating from 1906-1909, is the work of Vladimír Županský.

The Vinohrady Theatre was the second stone theatre to be built in Bohemia and brought to an end the monopoly of the National Theatre. From then on, Czech theatre enjoyed the practical possibility of competing for primacy within the same art form and the same language culture.

The construction of the theatre was implemented amidst a boom of creative and social activities. The first part of the Vinohrady Hospital was opened, as well as the Rieger Gardens; a covered market was built; and the driving of a tun-

The striking feature of the house at no. 1527/9 Na Švihance Street is this attractive portal with its wooden marquise and magnificent sculptures of crested peacocks

nel under Vyšehrad was began in 1902, the year in which the municipal council took a decision to build the Vinohrady Theatre. At the same time the racecourse in Velká Chuchle commenced its activities (the original buildings in Art Nouveau style have, unfortunately, been demolished); MCHAT appeared at the National Theatre for the first time; the first exhibition of "Osma" featuring the painters Filla, Kubín, Kubišta, Nowak and others was held and the Ponrepo, first permanent Czech cinema opened in Karlova Street in the Old Town.

This brief comment on the atmosphere of the period also explains the interest of the citizens of Vinohrady in having their own theatre, as the theatre absorbs, and is a sensitive part of, the atmosphere. The Vinohrady Theatre is still one of the most significant cultural centres of Prague and Bohemia. A whole range of prominent figures of Czech cultural life worked and appeared on stage in this building, where dozens of playwrights, dramatists, directors and designers also left their mark.

The built-up area behind the Vinohrady Theatre is the most striking evidence of the speedy development of Prague at the beginning of the 20th century. Entire streets in Vinohrady and Žižkov, as well as in Vršovice, Nusle, Karlín, Holešovice and Smíchov, illustrate a still remarkable phenomenon: the standard of building set by a talented generation of architects like Osvald Polívka or Josef Fanta is also reflected in the work of the builders and master masons who created the majority of Art Nouveau blocks of flats in these districts of Prague. The closer we get to náměstí Míru, formerly Purkyňovo Square, the more the houses reflect the standard architectonic Art Nouveau decoration - large recurring masks, and plaster wreaths with flowing ribbons.

The examples of the style may be found just around the corner from the Vinohrady Theatre, in Římská and Italská Streets. The house at no. 1199/35 Římská Street erected in 1903 by the architect and builder Karel Horák, is dominated by two figural sculptures impersonating building of houses. The house has remarkable loggias with beautiful grating and ceilings decorated with stylised plasterwork flowers. We should also notice house no. 1240/39, with only simple plaster ornaments and forged floral grating. On house no. 1223/20 in Italská Street, we can see a sign "V Černochově" and huge grinning masks under the ledge above the windows of the third floor, with plaster ribbons flowing down the ledge.

If we turn to the right at the first crossroads and walk along the wider Vinohrady Avenue (Vinohradská třída), we now have the Vinohrady Covered Market (Vinohradská tržnice) on our right. It is an glazed iron structure built in sober Nco-Renaissance style and designed by the architect Antonín Turek at the beginning of the 20th century. It is currently undergoing extensive reconstruction. Behind the Covered Market on our right, we see the Svatopluk Čech Gardens (Sady Svatopluka Čecha), containing a remarkable 1924 memorial by the sculptor Jan Štursa and the architect Pavel Janák. We should also pay attention to house no. 1485/63 on the left-hand side, built in 1907 by Josef Pospíšil, and no. 48/4, designed between 1912 and 1913 by Kotěra's co-worker, Otakar Novotný. As we are especially interested in Art Nouveau, we might now direct our gaze at an ornamented Gothic-Art Nouveau house at no. 1465/73, thus characterised by its compound windows and panels above the windows containing stucco decoration with floral motifs. On the other hand, the house no. 1216/87 called "U Jungmanna" is characterised by its abundant wreaths with ribbons and festoons, with masks and heraldic plates in between. The adjoining house no. 33/89 with masonry balconies and Art Nouveau surface plaster decoration (masks and floral décor) has a remarkable interior. The forged grating is made up of recurrent masks, the glass in the staircase windows is etched and the most beautiful of all are the doors to the flats. Their window panes are made of coloured mosaic patterns of thick glass, sealed in lead. All this is protected by a forged grating with an ornamental pattern.

We have now reached náměstí Jiřího z Poděbrad (George of Poděbrady Square), dominated by the Church of the Sacred Heart (kostel Nejsvětějšího srdce Páně). However, we continue to walk to the left until we reach the corner house no. 1552/14 (on the corner of the square and Mánesova Street), built in 1909, whose Art Nouveau façade faces onto the square. In the centre of the façade is an outstanding sculpture of George of Poděbrady; the gable is ornamented with the bird sculptures and big vases. Two bay windows with wooden pannelled loggias produce a charming impression. Under the main cornice of the lateral side of the house we can see a folk ornament in the painting. We also recommend a walk along Mánesova Street and its perpendicular streets U Kanálky and Třebízského to see the houses, many of which are of Art Nouveau character or have Art Nouveau - decorated façades. When approaching náměstí Jiřího z Poděbrad, we should have a look at Art Nouveau houses no. 1648/80, ornamented with geometrical patterns and coloured tiles, and no. 1563/77; in the case of house no. 1612/79, we should

notice its beautiful balcony grating and the masonry banisters of the side balconies. No. 1641/68 has a distinctly flat façade and finer stuccoed ornamentation, embellished by the oval shapes of the tiles. Houses no. 1633/74 and no. 1647/72 are more ornamental. The first one has intricately sculptured and finely treated cream-coloured stucco on grey plastering and a stunning forged spiral grating in the bay window loggia. In the interior there are window panes of etched glass and coloured rectangular glass. House no. 1647/72 has a more Gothic-Art Nouveau character, and its façade is decorated with beautiful relief scenes in rectangular frames. The wall tiling has been preserved inside the house, with the tiles combined into figural scenes. The corridors contain a stylised flower laid in mosaics of the flats windows. A stylised sunflower and a sun - both on the gable and on the bay window - are used as the main motif in the décor of house no. 1378/3 in U Kanálky Street, dating from 1906. The entrance is again guarded by mascarons and the appearance of balconies is embellished by plaster decoration and tiles. House no. 1359/4, dating from 1905, bears distinct elements of two styles-the Neo-Gothic and Art-Nouveau - and bears the name "Pod Křivoklátem". The richly segmented front with balconies is decorated by Art Nouveau circles with vegetal ornamentation.
Other houses with similar Art Nouveau decoration in historicising styles can be found in Mánesova Street and the adjoining Třebízského Street.

One of the most interesting streets in Vinohrady is undoubtedly Polská, which runs into Rieger Gardens (Riegerovy sady) from Italská Street, and on to the crossroads of Slavíčkova and Ondříčkova Streets. The whole street is a display of houses dating mostly from the 20th century, in historicising styles: lower down the street, there are Art Nouveau elements on the façades; further up, we find almost purely Art Nouveau and post-Art Nouveau houses. The street looks unusually interesting and sculpture-like from various angles, even exceptionally grandiose, which is very unusual in comparison with blocks of flats in other parts of suburbian Prague. Especially unique is the rich segmentation of façades, mainly by means of bay windows, which are, moreover, in many different places, have various shapes and in their upper parts penentrate the balcony loggias and arcades. The sculptural quality of the façades is also produced by the lavish figural decoration, bossing and ashlaring up to the first floor, step-like, mostly masonry or stone balconies of various sizes, attics, and variously shaped gables of the houses. The interiors are usually ornamented with etched window glass on the landings, marble facing of the entrance corridors, mirrors, tiled walls with Art Nouveau patterns, and mosaic tiles in the entrances and at each floor level.

Among older houses in Polská Street we should notice house no. 1283/18 called "U Assyrských králů"(The Assyrian Kings), dating from 1904. The sculptures surrounding the entrance are in keeping with the house's name. The house has a Neo-Renaissance character and Art Nouveau façade. Similarly, house no. 1260/24 is decorated with plasterwork reliefs and heraldic plates. Houses no. 1506/42 and 1505/40 synthethize Neo-Renaissance and Art Nouveau architecture in an interesting way. Alongside the first storey of house no. 1506/42 stretches a massive balcony on consoles with floral festoons, and a segmented bay window, with balconies and loggias ornamented with floral panelling decorated with stylised ornaments, rises upwards from the first floor.

House no. 32 has two symmetrically located bay windows in the central part of the façade; a dark plaster vegetal ornament around and below the bay windows is nicely accentuated by the light plastering. The interior of the house provides an example of the interior fittings in this district: the beautiful paving with floral ornamentation, masks, corridor windows decorated with plasterwork and gratings in the shape of stylised lillies, preserved original plates indicating floors, or spyholes. House no. 1565/3 is a typical three-axial house with slightly arched bay windows on lateral axes and massive covered balconies. There is a very similar house just next to it, no. 1509/5, through it has differently shaped balconies and bay windows. The central bay window is combined with balconies.

The large house at no. 1675/52 has outstanding masks above the windows and figural sculptures below the bay window. Along the sides of the bay windows we may observe narrow openings, even slots glazed with a coloured mosaic which produce a charming impression when lit up in the evening. The beautiful mosaic is repeated on a larger scale inside the house on the door panes on the mezzanines and on the windows in the flat. Equally impressive is the marble facing in the entrance corridor, which ends in a band of plasterwork ornaments below the ceiling. Above the marble facing is a wonderfully executed stuccoed panel ceiling. Just above the entrance, in the interior, we encounter a charming sculptural relief of the Madonna and Child. The Art Nouveau fittings are complemented with other details - the name plates, staircase grating or original mosaic tiling.

House no. 1618/9 outshines the others as a result of its forged balcony grating and the combination of smooth plastering and rough brickwork. The rectangles between the windows contain interesting figural reliefs of children

A multi-coloured reinforced glass mosaic and grille containing decorative spiral elements complement the remarkable interior of a block of flats at no. 33/89 Vinohradská Avenue

at play. On some houses, for example at no. 1621/11, the balcony railings are substituted for shaped pillars with oval ornaments. The three-axial house at no. 1673/13 is ornamented especially alongside its lateral, slightly arched bay windows, with vertical bands of geometrical ornaments, which are also repeated, with a few variations, on the plasterwork of the interior.

Retracing our steps only a few dozen metres, we turn to the right around the Rieger Gardens into Chopinova, where we may compare the Art Nouveau ornamentation of the façades with the rising stylistic modern movement as presented by the architect Jan Kotěra. Laichter House (Laichterův dům), no. 1543/4, dating from 1908-1909, already rejects the common naturalistic Art Nouveau ornamentation of that period, although it does not eliminate its decorative component. As the façade clearly shows, the plaster ornamentation on the façade is substituted for a variety of materials used. The rhythm of the verticals strips on the ground storey of the building and on the risalit which protrudes from the central part the first floor - is divided up in the upper storeys by a rhythm of horizontals in the form of brickwork bands and an inlaid main cornice. Brick, stone and variously treated plastering, as well as the glass in the large windows and painted parts of window frames, produce a grand decorative impression. With all its new functionalism and simplicity, the architecture is still mainly a means of expression, that is art. The neighbouring houses, no. 1556/6, dating from 1909-1910 and no. 1564/8, dating from 1909, were built in a similar style and include architectonic sculptures on the Ancient Egyptian model (. . . by the sculptor Antonín Waigant). Chopinova Street stretches along the Rieger gardens as far as Vozová Street. Besides other interesting houses, for example the beautiful Neo-Renaissance house at no. 1493/24 with a large Renaissance gable, we find Art Nouveau houses with beautiful stuccoed ornaments and masks such as those at no. 1472/ 14) or the four massive Neoclassicist masks above the main cornice of the house façade at no. 1478/22.

Nevertheless, the relatively short streets connecting Chopinova and Slavíkova look the most interesting and appealing. The first of them is Krkonošská. Right on the corner we see what is probably the oldest house in the street, no. 1474/1; it is Gothic-Renaissance in style, yet its façade displays typical Art Nouveau plaster ornaments and interesting animal mascarons. On the façade of house no. 1522/4, we should especially notice the outstanding stuccoed vegetal ornaments around pilasters along all sides of the entrance. Stuccoed vegetal ornaments can also be found between the windows on the floors. The richest plaster decoration is probably that of house no. 1534/6, especially below a step-like loggia and around the entrance. House no. 1557/8, dating from 1908, has a large corner figural sculpture. House no. 1623/12, built in 1911, is interesting because of its balconies, which have finely stuccoed banister panelling, sometimes in the shape of wreaths. The bay window of the house displays a figural relief; on the mezzanine windows we can see etched hunting scenes; and the staircase has a rich handrail grating. The Gothic-Art Nouveau house no. 1477/15 is also decorated with a beautiful forged grating on its balconies.

It is difficult to describe the individual apartment houses on Na Švihance. Every house in the street is interesting, and most façades bear elements of Art Nouveau decoration. No. 1776, a corner Gothic-Art Nouveau house with a tower, has a bossed corner and is decorated with a large sculpture of St. Hubert with a stag and a sundial. The pure Art Nouveau house at no. 1475/3 has an interesting timber frame on the gable and a wooden marquise in the central part of the façade along the axis of the house. House no. 1550/4 differs from the others because of its asymmetrically placed gables, and house no. 1527/9 belongs to the Art Nouveau style as a result of its sculptures of peafowl around the entrance.

Houses on Vozová, the street which lead us into Slavíkova Street, also contain some Art Nouveau elements. In Slavíkova, the façades on the Vinohrady side of the street look more interesting, but the Žižkov side also contains some fine decorations. For example, house no. 1047/10 displays not only the freshness of a renovated façade, but also contains three huge mascarons below the main cornice and a portal ornamented with stuccoed branches and fruit.

Art Nouveau and post-Art Nouveau houses with less abundant decoration on relatively flat façades, were built on Kubelíkova and Bořivojova Streets. Furthermore, we can take a look at the previously mentioned Jewish Cemetery in Fibichova Street and retrace our steps to Jiřího z Poděbrad Square. From here we walk along the bottom of the square to the Vinohrady Water-Tower (Vinohradská vodárna) at no. 725, built in Neo-Renaissance style in 1891 by the architect Antonín Turek. Next to it rises the slender bell-tower of a constructivist structure dating from the thirties by the architect Pavel Janák - Husův sbor církve československé (the Czechoslovak Hussite Church Choir).

As we walk below the park along Slovenská ulice, we arrive at an interesting villa, no. 1566, containing the studio of Ladislav Šaloun, who built it on his own design in 1910.

The exterior of the villa is typically Art Nouveau, with high sculpturally decorated windows. Besides a large stu-

The oriel window of an Art Nouveau building located at
no. 1475/3 Na Švihance Street
in Vinohrady

Apartment blocks in Vinohrady are decorated down to the most minute detail, as this small owl on a building in Chopinova Street demonstrates

One of the interesting buildings (no. 1556/6) on Chopinova Street in Vinohrady, dating from 1909. Its sculptor, Antonín Waigant, was an exponent of austere modernism at that time

dio, the interior includes a nicely furnished, typically country-style room. Nowadays the studio houses the Ladislav Šaloun gallery.

In nearby Hradešínská Street, we reach another interesting villa no. 1542/6, belonging to Jan Kotěra. The building exemplifies the advanced stage of the modern movement and Czech functionalism between 1908-1909. It lacks almost any ornamental elements and applies the texture of the building material instead. We saw a similar example with the Laichter House in Chopinova Street. Our longer walk ends here. The simplest way in which to return to the centre is to go back to Jiřího z Poděbrad Square and take the underground back to Wenceslas Square.

The panels in the balustrade, the charming stucco work and the figural relief on the oriel window of house no. 1623/12 (Krkonošská Street), constructed in 1911, captivate the onlooker

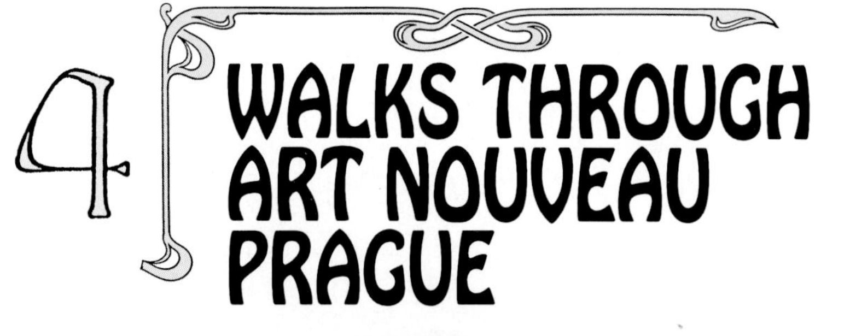

4 WALKS THROUGH ART NOUVEAU PRAGUE

The design for the Štěpánek family gravestone in section VI-10b of the Olšany Cemeteries was created by Jan Kotěra and used by metallist Václav Mašek to craft the bronze relief

A walk around the largest Prague cemeteries should not induce a morose mood, but rather show the visitor that sacred places can be a source of much enlightenment concerning art and architecture. Almost all architects and sculptors paid homage through their art to prominent deceased personalities by means of statues, sculptures or the architectonic treatment of tombstones. Funeral creations, therefore, form a considerable part of their work.

The work of architects, sculptors, builders, stonemasons and metal founders can be seen especially in the Olšany Cemeteries (Olšanské hřbitovy), the largest burial place in Prague, and in the nearby New Jewish Cemetery (Nový židovský hřbitov). The simplest and most rapid connection between the two is the underground: take line A from the centre to Flora Station, and walk for just a few minutes along Vinohradská Avenue.

The name of the Olšany Cemeteries commemorates the old settlement of Olšany, a place where at the beginning of the 14th century there stood a farm with a lake and vineyard. In 1679 the then owner sold an extensive garden to the Old Town municipality for the purpose of burying victims of the plague. Soon afterwards the Churches of St. Roch, St. Sebastian and St. Rosalie were built in the new cemetery. The construction was approved by the Archbishop of Prague Jan Bedřich, Count of Wallenstein. Thus, in about 1680 the first Olšany Cemetery began to expand around the church, and was again filled with victims of the plague. In 1713-1714, and again in 1771-1772, the cemetery was filled with plague victims. In 1787 Emperor Joseph II decided to ban burials in cemeteries around the parish churches in inner Prague, and the Prague municipality decided that Olšany should become the central cemetery for the whole of Prague lying on the right bank of the Vltava. Since then, the area of the Olšany cemeteries has increased several times to cover currently about 50 hectares, and contains about 110,000 graves.

The cemeteries are divided into ten sectors. The oldest, section I, around the Church of St. Roch, with the oldest graves and tombstones, was abolished, and is now only accessible from sections II to X. Those wishing to see funeral works of the Art Nouveau epoch should head for sections IV to IX. To the left of the main entrance we see the biggest memorial of the Olšany cemeteries, built for the family of the court counsellor, Alois Hrdlička. In 1900 their only son Jan, a student of the consular academy, was buried here. The group of life-size statues is by the sculptor František Rous, who also created many other tombstones. The epitaph on the tombstone is in French and reads (in translation) as follows:

The memorial to the great painter Luděk Marold at the Olšany Cemeteries was adorned by Vilém Amort with a bronze sculptural relief in 1904

Josef Fanta designed this tombstone at the New Jewish Cemetery, where Bohumil Bondy was buried in 1907

"When the day closes and I fall into sleep, come to see my grave. But only look and do not cry too much, for the who sleeps likes to dream, and at close of day the silent night is sweet."

Close to the left, in section VI-6b, we find the impressive grave of Josef Kodl (1909). Its tombstone is in Art Nouveau style and is made up of a tiered marble tombstone, on which a huge broken tree with dead leaves had fallen. The author of this highly emotional bronze sculpture is also František Rous, and it was built by the firm of Pupp and Škarka. The broken tree, symbolic and typical of funeral sculptures of that period, embodies death and grief.

By the wall separating sections V and VI, immediately to the right, lies buried one of the prominent Czech painters of the end of the 19th century, Luděk Marold, the author of the famous three-dimensional panorama of the Battle of Lipany, situated in a pavillon in the Exhibition Grounds (Výstaviště). Marold drew experience from his stays in Munich and Paris and was a great illustrator and graphic artist, as well as an author of oil paintings. He worked his way to fame especially through illusionist illustrations. Marold's memory was honoured by the sculptor Vilém Amort, who also participated in the decoration of Prague's Municipal House (Obecní dům), with a bronze tombstone relief in 1904. The relief pictures the painter's portrait with a palette and a grieving woman (Marold's wife, Zdeňka, was also buried here in 1903). The memorial was ordered by the Prague Union of Artists. We should also note the next tombstone in Art Nouveau style. It is a tomb slab of Anna E. Grohmann, created in 1905 (. . . by the sculptor Josef Mauder) with the participation of the metal founder Václav Mašek from Karlín. The bronze relief represents an angel, and stylised bronze flowers are laid on the tomb slab.

The same section contains the tomb of Karel Maydl, a university professor and surgeon. The architect of this monumental black marble tomb with a huge interwoven bronze wreath was Jan Kotěra, and it was decorated by the sculptor Bohumil Kafka.

Behind the dividing wall, in section IV-9, we find the tombstone of Josef Fanta (died 1954), a well-known Art Nouveau architect, made to his own design. Fanta was also a designer of the Main Railway Station in Prague. A circular relief of the Madonna and Child is framed with stylised branches and cones. A bronze bust of Dr. Antonín Frič (1913), a university professor of zoology, was created by Bohumil Kafka: it is located in section IV-7.

In section VI-16, by the dividing wall, are monumental and lavishly decorated tombs. Among them is a memorial to the family of Vojtěch Mastný, a director of Živnobanka; the academic sculptor, František Rous, created a statue of a mourning woman in a classical robe sculptured in stone. Here we discern another feature of Art Nouveau décor - the pillars are coiled with spirals, the vases with flowers stand on the top of the tomb, and we can also see a peacock's tail open into the form of a fan. The whole tomb was built by the firm of Jan Rada and son. Nearby we immediately notice the Novák family tombstone. On the black tombstone with a white cross is a bronze sculpture of Christ, encircled by a huge bay wreath, and the corners are adorned with a coloured vegetable mosaic. Voluminous flower pots decorated with reliefs of child figures also represent an interesting work of sculpture. This tomb in Art Nouveau style was created in 1901 by Bedřich Bendelmayer and the Červenka firm.

The tombstone of the Štěpánek family in section VI-10b stands out from the composition of previous memorials. It was designed by Jan Kotěra, and the bronze relief was made on his design by the metal founder Václav Mašek. On top of the monument, in a wrought arch, is a bronze angel with a gilded tiara, with flowing ribbons and wings. Around a simply shaped stylised figure, ornaments coil in both directions. The flower pots also contain a typically Art Nouveau floral motif. Another of Kotěra's works may be observed on the next tombstone, to the actor Eduard Vojan and his family. The monument was created by Václav Žďárský in 1903, on the basis of Kotěra's design. This pair of sculptors also participated in the creation of a tombstone bearing the inscription "Jakub Vojta Slukov, actor and playwright" (1903) in the same row. It is a simple granite tombstone entwined with a huge fallen oak made of sandstone. The sculptor and stonemason, Václav Žďárský, was the author of many Art Nouveau tombstones and he himself has a grave in section VI-8, decorated with the sandstone figure of a woman by Alex Zelinka. The work of the famous sculptor Stanislav Sucharda can be observed on the tombstone of the painter Mařenka Dostálová (1903). A male figure in a simple folklore costume leans against a slender tombstone with a relief portrait of the deceased.

In section VIII-1 is a tombstone of the famous painter Antonín Slavíček (1910), created by Josef Mařatka and presented by the Mánes group for Slavíček's lifelong work and dissemination of Czech art abroad (amongst other accolades, in 1900 he was awarded a bronze medal for his work at the World Exhibition in Paris).

In section IX-17 we should notice a high slender tombstone containing an owl and hands - the grave of J. B.

An impressive symbolic Art Nouveau gravestone in the form of a broken tree by sculptor František Rous, on the tomb of Josef Kodl at the Olšany Cemeteries

Lambl (1909), a professor at the Czech Technical University. Another of Sucharda's works, a bronze sculpture of a woman with the title "Mother is leaving", can be seen on the tomb of the Štěpánek family (1913) in section IX-12. The composer J. B. Foerster is buried in a family tomb which is located in section IX-2; the sculptor Vilém Amort was the author of the memorial dating from 1907 with a portrait on a background of St. Vitus Cathedral. Finally, we can have (IX-1) a look at a bronze tombstone relief by František Bílek from 1929 on a monument commissioned by the Czech Academy of Science and Art for the well-known sculptor, Josef Mauder. It bears the inscription "The moment of creation embraces one's whole life".

The New Jewish Cemetery is very close to this sacred place. As we walk out of the Olšany Cemeteries, we turn to the left, cross Jana Želivského before the crossroads and opposite Želivského metro station walk into the gateway of the New Jewish Cemetery. If you do not have something with which to cover your head, it can be borrowed from the guard at the entrance. The cemetery was founded in 1891 and contains functional buildings, such as a ceremonial hall with a chapel, rooms for the preparation of funerals, an administrative building and the burial ground itself, which has the capacity to hold about 100 000 graves. The cemetery has its places and memorials of honour. In the centre of the space by the main alley is a burial ground destined as the last resting place of those who have made the greatest contribution to Jewish unity, and at the entrance to the cemetery the remains of important rabbis are buried. Also at the entrance a memorial was installed (1985) to the victims of the ship called The Patria, together with one to the Czechoslovak Jews who died in concentration camps or were killed in combat.

Among the most important architects who created tombstones in the New Jewish Cemetery is Jan Kotěra. Eminent works of Art Nouveau funeral architecture are represented by the graves of Nathan Robitschek's family and the Elbogen family in the second section near the cemetery wall. The large tomb of the Elbogen family, from 1901, is surprising in its lack of ornamentation, accentuating the expressive quality of the noble dark stone. It has a typical triple composition, creating the impression of the gateway of death. The round marble flower pots which decorate the corners of the granite plinth are also interesting. Vegetal ornaments and Art Nouveau curves were applied only on the intricate grating of a low gate at the front of the tomb. The next tomb, of Nathan Robitschek's family, from 1901-1902, contrasts with the first, and enables us to compare Kotěra's works. It has a more picturesque character, and sculptural architectonic elements of light stone contribute to its almost sculptural nature. Sculptured ornamental flowers stand out on the capital of the tombstone, on two lower supporting pillars and on two equal pillars in the front of the tomb separated by a metal door with a recurrent floral décor. Both tombs are complete architectonic works of art showing Kotěra's search for expression. In 1902 Kotěra created another work of art in Art Nouveau style for the grave of Egon Heinrich Perutz at the end of row 7-5. A tall, slender white tombstone ends in a pointed arch and contains a fine relief vegetal ornamentation. Another of Kotěra's outstanding works, in the late Art Nouveau style dating from 1904, can be found on the Perutz grave in row 11-1. Around the grave is a profiled black granite border with a little step, the tombstone with the names of the deceased ending in decorative extensions with consoles and a coloured frieze.

Another important architect, Adolf Zasche, designed two graves by the other wall. The Thorsch grave from 1908 is an excellent Art Nouveau work. A high stone balustrade with columns borders the grave. Forged panels bear simple geometrical ornamentation. The grave called Götz, a post-Art Nouveau tomb from 1911, was worked out conceptually and completed with features displaying a high quality of art and craftsmanship.

In about 1907 a prominent architect of the Czech Art Nouveau, Josef Fanta, designed the tomb (in section 7) of an industrialist and supporter of Czech-Jewish religious endeavours, Bohumil Bondy. The extensive gravestone consists of a body made from granite slabs, on which there are five marble gravestone panels. On the central slab there is a huge wreath with the name of the deceased written inside it. Bronze decoration, also with the names of the deceased written inside it, separates the side slabs. A smaller bronze slab bears a Hebrew text. A grass area in front of the gravestone has columns at its corners, and there are granite benches along both sides. Fanta's design was executed by the master stonemason, Eduard Radnitz.

A unique example of the Art Nouveau design of a gravestone is the grave of the painter Max Horb, from 1907, in section 19-1-13 in the main alley. The monument was created by the famous Czech sculptor, Jan Štursa, apparently taking up Horb's model of the sandstone grave-

The black marble tombstone of Karel Maydl, designed by Jan Kotěra, at the Olšany Cemeteries. Bohumil Kafka crafted the bronze wreaths and ribbons

Jan Štursa created this Art Nouveau gravestone (1907) of painter Max Horb at the New Jewish Cemetery

stone - the relief of a weeping willow dominated by a peacock with a drooping tail.

The late Art Nouveau gravestone of Rabbi Ehrenfeld by the architect Paul Albert Kopetzký from 1912 stands at the entrance to section 5-B. The huge sarcophagus is adorned with post-Art Nouveau style decoration, architecture and script of extraordinary quality. At the beginning of section 5-B-1-3 we find Sophie Pollak's grave. This is a unique example of Viennese Art Nouveau in this cemetery, executed by the architect E. V. Gotthilf in around 1899. On the pedestal a high square obelisk stands with a cornice edge displaying a bronze girdle with rosettes and a segment with vegetal decoration. In the upper third there is a girdle ornamented with a meander with four brackets with wreaths. The Art Nouveau design here has an Imperial basis.

The monumental tomb, first in the row at the main path of the cemetery, in section 5-B-1-1-2, with the inscription of the Weltsch family, is a protected monument. It was designed by Art Nouveau architect Antonín Balšánek in 1900 and comprises a square granite mausoleum with two Doric columns and a dome. Bronze festoons hang along the sides. Under them there is a three-part window. Decorative forged lattice doors and three stairs with two ornamental side vases lead to the entrance. The grave was also built by stonemason Eduard Radnitz.

In section B-3-14-8, 9 we find the Sommer grave from 1901. In the alcove of the grave is a relief plaque with a portrait of the deceased. Nearby, in section 3-B-13-11, we can admire the Art Nouveau Löwy tomb from 1900 with an oblong gravestone on a pedestal, wreaths and hangers. It is unique for its style as well as its art.

Art Nouveau marked out several other remarkable gravestones from the years 1901-1911. In section 7-1-1 we notice the exemplary, simple architecture of the Gerstl gravestone, with two flower pots. The gravestone of Louise Russ (section 7-1-12), in the shape of stylised vegetal volutes, is made from white granite. It differs fundamentally from other Art Nouveau gravestones. The remarkable decoration will draw one's attention to the grave at the end of row 7-1 (Jenny Pollak). This is an example of Art Nouveau vegetal decoration. On the right, the grave of David Bunzl--Federn from 1903, a Art Nouveau work conspicuous for its modest decoration on a rounded-off marble gravestone, draws one's attention.

On the other hand the next grave, that of Albert Fanta from 1913, is a standard Art Nouveau gravestone with a decorative extension and a typical metal balustrade. A plaque, perhaps made by A. Rieber, on the grave of

A most unusual Art Nouveau tombstone, that of Louise Russ, displays stylised vegetal volutes and is to be found at the New Jewish Cemetery

J. Herrnheiser in section 7-8-36,is very similar to the works of sculptor Stanislav Sucharda.

The second grave from the end of row 8-1 (Roth), with a granite gravestone and a decorative bronze flower pot, is late Art Nouveau style work typically in every aspect. The architect Josef Zasche created another gravestone in section 11-1-8, 9, bearing the name Krasnopolski. A kind of small temple with bronze columns has a triangular gable and in the middle of it a slab bearing the names of the deceased. Areas are decorated with rich linear vegetal motifs, and a metal grave lantern hangs on chains under the lintel. At the end of row 12-15 we find a grave bearing the name Kraus; it has an Art Nouveau composition with pleasant art and craft elements, for instance quadratic flower pots. However, the grave is badly damaged. The grave bearing the name of Karoline Heller in section 15-14-13, on which stylised decorations run out from frontal stone flower pots onto the side of a high gravestone, is a foremost monumental Art Nouveau composition. The architect Adolf Foehr created a gravestone in row 15-1 bearing the name Therese Sohr. It has a strictly proportional composition, a higher full granite balustrade and little frontal bronze doors. Along the sides are a couple of prismatic columns with opened semi-circular heads like flower pots. A gravestone from about 1910 inscribed with the name of Reinisch, a high granite pylon of elliptical ground plan with a bronze locket of the deceased and a yashmak in the upper part, stands in plot 19-1-3.

Besides these famous graves and tombs with Art Nouveau decoration or architecture, there is a whole row of other graves in the New Jewish Cemetery where Art Nouveau decoration is routinely employed. We will find them for instance in section 15-1 (Neugröschel, Klemprer, Vilhelm Lutzer), in section 15-14-9 - Friedrich Wehle - or in section 16-4, with the inscription Rosa Mahler, as well as in other sections. When visiting the New Jewish Cemetery we cannot miss the opportunity of seeing the grave of the writer Franz Kafka in section 21-14-21, a protected monument partly because of its artistic value. The gravestone has the shape of a six-sided crystal with details of the deceased on the front. Its author was the architect L. Ehrmann.

We now set out from the New Jewish Cemetery down Vinohradská Avenue as far as the Vinohrady Cemetery where Jan Kotěra, among others, is buried, then continue along Černokostelecká Street as far as the early 20th century villa situated on the left-hand side of the street. Three different villas show how the Art Nouveau style was expressed in the building of standard family houses. Villa Zdeňka at no. 207/1 protrudes onto the street with a wider front and a longer lower wing with a garret window and a little tower. The flat façade is decorated with a combination of parget and plaster. The Art Nouveau ornamental decoration appears only under the window cornices. A verandah, above which is a terrace with a grid of geometrical shapes, is annexed to the house. Villa no. 206/3 has a more complicated composition with a tower and a front gable on which darker stucco ornaments are situated, and with a side gable under which a verandah is located. The construction was carried out by J. A. Smolík, a master builder from Strašnice. House no. 179/13, from 1908, is a one-floor villa with a bay window on a relatively low front facing the street. The house is set back in a quieter part of the garden. The Art Nouveau decoration is limited to stucco wreaths.

Along the street, vertically opposite the villas, we reach Vešínova Street where we find a whole row of blocks of flats built in Art Nouveau style for less wealthy occupants. So, for instance, nos. 222/9 and 11 are two identical blocks of flats built by František Sedláček, a master bricklayer, with gables above the side axes and entrances, and a façade divided with a different plaster. House no. 184/8 is similar, differing only in the richer decoration on the side gable where a vine motif dominates. Similarly, even house 202/3 has the same Art Nouveau decorative ornaments.

We cross Starostrašnická from Vešínova Street into Vilová Street, in which Villa Trmal no. 91/11, Jan Kotěra's creation from 1902, is worth seeing. The architect, when building, drew upon Czech folk architecture ingeniously. The simple little villa has a plain gable panelled with wood and a carved wooden balustrade. Other villas in this street are worth taking a look at, for instance no. 17, or no.14, Villa Criola. We now return to Starostrašnická from Vilová Street as far as the underground station, from where we return to the city centre.

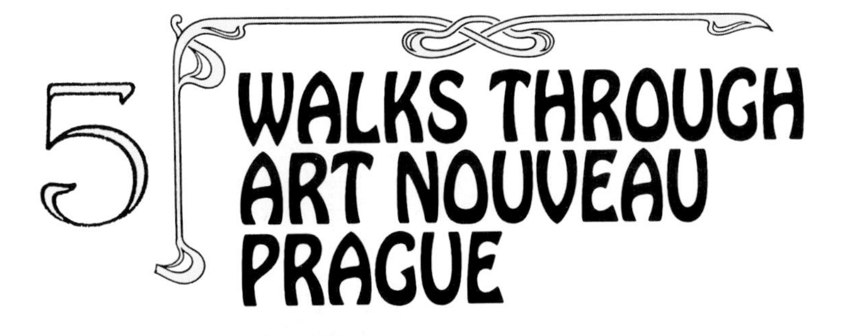

5 WALKS THROUGH ART NOUVEAU PRAGUE

A detail from the decoration in the Mayorial Hall in the Municipal House: the ornamental capital of a mirror

The most famous Art Nouveau Prague structure, to which it is necessary to devote a separate chapter, is the Municipal House (Obecní dům or Reprezentační dům), built as a dignified representative building of the town. The Prague municipality reacted to the growing cultural needs of its citizens from the beginning of the century and had a splendid modern place for social life built on the boundary of Na Příkopě Street and náměstí Republiky (Republic Square), in the vicinity of the Powder Tower (Prašná brána).

In 1903 a public architectural competition for the best design for a Municipal House building for the city of Prague at the request of Měšťanská beseda (The Patrician Society) was organized. However, designs appraised by Alois Dryák, Josef Pospíšil and Antonín Balšánek were adjudged to be of equal merit. As even a second competition for the best design, to which Osvald Polívka was also invited, did not lead to a decision, in the end Antonín Balšánek was awarded the job. He was professor Schulze's pupil and

The Municipal House of the city of Prague, erected on a design by architect Antonín Balšánek and Osvald Polívka between 1905 and 1912

therefore also a prominent expert in Neo-Renaissance and Neo-Baroque architecture. Osvald Polívka was included in the team in recognition of the results he had achieved at the turn of the century in designs of public as well as private buildings, and this not only in Prague. He created remarkable interiors in which, as was the case with other national and social buildings - such as the Zemská banka (from 1894-1896, built in the style of the Czech Renaissance, with paintings by Max Švabinský in the vestibule) situated at no. 20 Na Příkopě, or the Hasičská Insurance Company in the Old Town Square - Neo-Baroque and eclectic shapes dominated for various reasons, often because of pressure exerted by master builders. Yet the main designer of the Municipal House was Antonín Balšánek, who based his design on a ground plan designed for the competition by Alois Dryák.

Construction commenced on 21 August 1905, and on 5 January 1912 the building was officially opened to the public. In charge of the actual construction work was the building firm F. Schlaffer and J. Šebek. The design of the building was carried out symmetrically on the basis of the diagonal shape of the building site, with an area of 4,200 square metres. The irregular shape of the site was designed in such a way that the first floor wings above the high ground floor come together at the central, sculpted entrance to the Municipal House, enclosed by a high dome.

The inscription in the photograph runs thus: "Success to you, Prague! Defy time, defy malice. May you withstand every tumult!

A mosaic entitled A Tribute to Prague, by Karel Špillar, is located on the central wing of the main façade, in the arched gable between the statues created by Ladislav Šaloun that represent the allegories Subduing of the Nation and Resurgence of the Nation. The sculptural decoration of the façade was created by Karel Novák and the bronze statues on the canopy were cast according to his design. The statues on the side walls were crafted by Antonín Mára, Josef Mařatka and František Úprka. The figure of Matěj Rejsek on the corner opposite the Powder Tower was created by Čeněk Vosmík.

The back of the Municipal House has conceptually speaking, the most important feature in a circular tower wing on the boundary line of both its wings, where the statue decoration is concentrated too. Statues of a Bagpiper and a Water Nymph (Rusalka) by František Úprka are expressively heartfelt and artistically symbolic. The attic sculptures Music and Drama by Josef Mařatka complete the composition of the architecture by means of their location and movement.

The Smetana Hall, the central space of the Municipal House, able to hold about 1,500 seated visitors, is situated in the middle of the first floor of the building. The decoration of the hall responds to its symbolism. Allegorical sculptoral groups entitled "Czech Dances" and "My Country" created by Ladislav Šaloun are placed along the sides of the dais; the ceiling paintings were created by František Ženíšek and the sculptures by Václav Novák. Karel Špillar was the author of the wall paintings Music, Dance, Poetry and Drama. The corpus of the organ, bearing a locket of Bedřich Smetana, was created by František Hergesel, and the portrait lockets of other composers by Josef Kalvoda. The author of the design of the Smetana Hall, as well as the exterior of the building, was Antonín Balšánek.

On the ground floor a spacious cloakroom is situated. Osvald Polívka, the author of the main façade, designed other representative restaurant and business rooms, too, and placed them in the wings of the building.

The beautifully decorated marquise which covers the main entrance into the Municipal House provides the visitor with a foretaste of the exquisite interior

Paintings by Alfons Mucha adorn the Mayorial Hall. The decoration of the vaults portrays the civic virtues, represented by figures from Czech history

The Grégr Hall, designed by Osvald Polívka and painted by František Ženíšek. The wall decoration is entitled "Song of Love, War and Burial"

The Mayorial Hall. The artistic ceiling decoration pictured here, the work of Alfons Mucha, shows a mythical eagle soaring above human figures and fruit trees

A curtain pull, a beautiful detail on the curtain itself, at the entrance to the Mayorial Hall

The Rieger Hall, designed by Osvald Polívka and decorated by Max Švabinský.
Josef Václav Myslbek sculpted the bust of
František Ladislav Rieger

The omnipresent Art Nouveau motif, the owl, can be found also in the Municipal House. This example is surrounded by the essential floral decoration

A sculpture of a nymph in white Carrara marble by Josef Pekárek, in the café at the Municipal House

The corridors in the Municipal House make the building fully accessible. The right-hand corridor on the ground floor leads to the Sladkovský Hall. The original stucco decoration and Art Nouveau metal and glass light fittings have been preserved in most of the Municipal Houses's interiors.

The Rieger Hall (František Rieger's bust was crafted by Josef Václav Myslbek) is superior to the others because of its paintings by Max Švabinský of prominent Czech writers and artists. The hall is also richly decorated with stucco figures and furnished with original Art Nouveau furniture. Other halls bear the names of significant Czech revivalists.

The Palacký Hall, in which the huge decorative paintings by Jan Preisler are the central feature, the Grégr Hall, the Božena Němcová Hall and the Oriental Hall are located in the Municipal House.

However, the Mayorial Hall outshines all the others. This circular room is vaulted by a dome with paintings by Alfons Mucha in the central circle, three stays and sectors of the painting. The scheme of Mucha's decoration, applying allegorical and symbolic pictures with expressive patriotic content depicting civic virtues, portrays personalities from Czech history and culminates in an impressive ceiling picture, in which a mythical eagle, its wings outspread, flies out of a circle portraying folk figures at work and a fruit tree in bloom. Three large windows face Republic Square and in the middle a door leads onto the terrace. The semi-circular portal with figures by Alfons Mucha is a grandiose element of the Mayorial Hall's ornaments. The capitals, or rather the mascarons, with the crowned head of a girl, a symbol of Prague, ornamented with laurel leaves, also attract attention.

Mucha's paintings provoked much discussion in his time, but now the Mayorial Hall ranks among the most valuable artistic monuments, thanks to its paintings. The Slovácký Hall, which is entered from the Božena Němcová Hall, is interesting, too. Its ceiling is adorned with stucco decoration. An Art Nouveau aquarium with brass ornaments is placed here as a focus of interest.

The ground-floor tearoom is noted for its white and gold interior, inspired by the Empire. Other rooms on the ground floor, as well as in the basement, serve as restaurants - the Pilsen restaurant, a bar, a wine bar,

The tearoom at the Municipal House is a combination of white and gold, the inspiration for which was drawn from the Empire. Osvald Polívka was the architect, and Václav Novák worked on the stucco decoration

"Prague receives its guests" by Josef Wenig,
in the French restaurant at the
Municipal House

"Viticulture" by Josef Wenig, in the French restaurant at the Municipal House

and a French restaurant situated to the right of the hall. Jakub Obrovský, Jaroslav Panuška, Václav Jansa and Roman Havelka decorated it. To the left of the entrance is a coffee lounge, at the far of which is a large recess panelled with green marble, dominated by a lighted fountain with a statue of a Nymph by Josef Pekárek, standing on a raised dais. The decoration of the hall is equally striking especially the reliefs of Fauna and Flora by Bohumil Kafka.

The Municipal House has served as a monument to Prague and the entire Czech nation since it was built. A whole series of prominent Czech artists worked on its decoration, paying tribute to the historical personalities of the Czech nation and the city of Prague. Without a doubt, the Smetana Hall is, historically speaking, the most significant room in the Municipal House. It was here that, in January 1918, the representatives of the Czech lands issued the so-called Declaration of the Three Kings demanding independence

The Grégr Hall at the Municipal House, with ceiling decoration by František Ženíšek

One of the beautiful stained-glass windows in the Rieger Hall at the Municipal House

The Palacký Hall at the Municipal House. The ceiling paintings were executed by Jan Preisler

for their country, and on 28 October of that year the first laws of the Czechoslovak Republic were proclaimed within its walls. The hall was also the scene of the spectacular events of November 1989. Music lovers know the Smetana Hall as the venue for concerts by prominent musicians from the Czech Republic and abroad, but first and foremost for the Prague Spring music festival.

The Municipal House, the most famous Art Nouveau building in Prague, continues to serve the purpose, for which it was designed by its founders. Opinions of experts on architectural design and the "over-decoration" of the Municipal House differ, and its main creators - Antonín Balšánek and Osvald Polívka - have already suffered much criticism for a long time. It remains a fact that the Municipal House, since it was opened, is regarded as an exhibition piece of artists and artistic craftsmen from the Art Nouveau period.

The foyer of the Municipal House. The bronze relief was created by the sculptor Bohumil Kafka

The Smetana Hall at the Municipal House. The stucco decoration relief work was entrusted by Václav Novák

The Smetana Hall. A detail from the sculptural and stucco decoration by Václav Novák, with a painting by Karel Špillar in the background

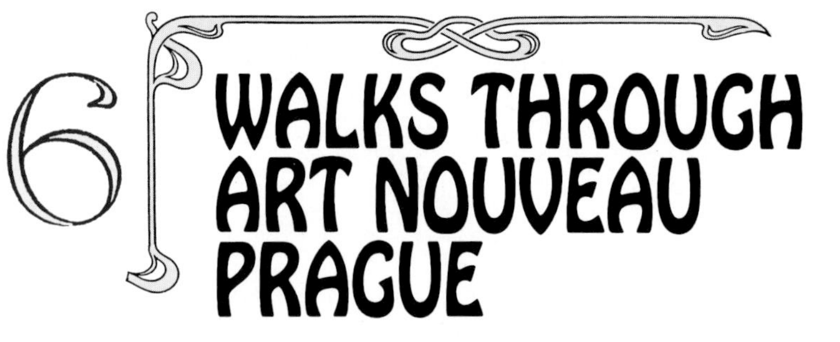

6 WALKS THROUGH ART NOUVEAU PRAGUE

A detail from the stucco decoration on an Art Nouveau building at no. 1078 on the corner of Celetná and U Prašné brány Streets

This walk takes in an interesting part of the Old Town, where slums had already been partially cleared by the turn of the century and new houses and whole streets have appeared alongside older buildings. Let us stop first of at the so-called Štenc House at No. 931/8, hidden from uninformed visitors to Prague behind the high nave in Salvátorská Street (we shall reach this structure, the Church of the Holy Saviour from the beginning of the 17th century, from Pařížská Avenue, when turning right into Kostečná Street. At first glance it stands out from all surrounding buildings, especially because of its façade whose sober nature is emphasised by an area of unplastered brick masonry. The house is an example of the reaction that took place against decorative Art Nouveau in the following period of architectural development, known as modernism. Hence the façade

A beautiful mosaic window as seen frequently in Prague buildings. This example shows the Art Nouveau representation of a peacock at the house called U Tří mušketýrů (The Three Musketeers)

These two massive eclectic corner houses bearing Art Nouveau decoration guard the entrance to V Kolkovně Street

does not include the traditional stucco floral motif and masks generally seen on Art Nouveau buildings. The graphic and architectural intentions are achieved by means of the building material used, and the contrast are created through the use of colour. A varied structure of masonry replaces sculptural ornaments, in the case of the Štenc House a contrast of red and whitish-grey brick. The house was built in 1909-1911 by Kotěra's co-worker, Otakar Novotný, as a residential house and as a studio for the editor Jan Štenc.

We now set out from Salvátorská Street to the crossroads of V Kolkovně, Dušní and Vězeňská Streets, where several blocks of flats draw our attention. Corner house no. 9 is almost the same as the second corner house, no. 910/2, called the Spear, on the corner of V Kolkovně and Vězeňská Streets. Both eclectical blocks of flats, crowned with in a tower corner, boast rich Art Nouveau stucco decoration on their façades. They are noteworthy first of all for their quantity of towers and turrets. Both houses are symmetrically situated in the two streets. V Kolkovně Street affords a view of richly divided house façades. It is true that their origin is Neo-Renaissance or Neo-Baroque; however, Art Nouveau decoration characterises houses such as no. 910/3, from 1905, with Art Nouveau paintings of scenes from Czech history and pictures with vegetal motifs.

At the crossroads of these streets we encounter a corner house, The Three Musketeers, at no.124/15. It is true that it is not Art Nouveau in style when judged according to its structure, yet it remains of interest. This is a standard house in this "better" part of the town, built by its owner, the architect František Niklas. Its preserved original details are remarkable. The lift lattice, for instance, is original, as are the lattice of the skylight and the cornerstone; the doors, with figures placed above them, have also been preserved. The largest ornament of the interior entrance area is a window with a fairy tale motif on the staircase landing including a lovely peacock formed from coloured glass.

From the next house, no. 135/7, situated in the Elišky Krásnohorské Street, a line of major post-Art Nouveau blocks of flats (postdating 1910) begins. Their little arched bays are similar to one another, and form a wave when viewed from the street. From the right-hand side the small street "U Svatého Ducha" (The Holy Ghost) leads into the Elišky Krásnohorské Street, where our attention is drawn to two corner houses built during the First World War; house no. 9/3, from 1915, bears its master builder's

name, Zákostelna, on the corner, as well as of its owner, Hovorka.

A dominant feature to the left of the house in Elišky Krásnohorské Street the red façade of house no. 135/7, built by Bohuslav Homoláč in 1910-1911. The two architectural sculptures of Hercules are striking. They carry bay windows on their loins and are connected to a bulky wreath. In fact, sculptures of Hercules often appear in this part of the Old Town on older, as well as newer houses. Big vases stand on the half-columns around the entrance and this creates a stronger overall impression when entering the house.

We cannot pass by the corner house no. 122/6 (on the corner of Elišky Krásnohorské and Bílkova Streets) without comment; the beautiful pottery ornaments on its bays, along the sides of the entrance, as well as among the windows and on the corner, draw our attention and create waved oval shapes. The little roofs above the balconies on bays, a motif of a spiral on the portal and on the lattice at the entrance are impressive. Its master builder, Josef Kovařovič, expressively divided the house, dating from 1912, by means of floor and parapet cornices. The combination of the plaster and parget also contributes to the decoration. Inside, an original chandelier, standing over the entrance staircase, has been preserved.

Part of typical vegetal stucco decoration on the gable of house no. 914/9 at the corner of Kozí and Vězeňská Streets

We now proceed along Bílkova Street as far as house no. 864/13, 15. Even from far off, our attention is drawn to a central bay and bulky gable, on which sits a sign of Prague in a different type of plaster. The inscription with waved bands proclaims "God Bless Work". The house, built in 1905, is interesting because of its two entrances situated on the side axes. Here we can observe the influence of Art Nouveau decoration on an older style. The next house, no. 855/19, erected in 1907, was a printing office, as striking inscription placed on it informs us. The façade of the Art Nouveau house is decorated with a combination of plaster and parget, oval shape and forged parapet protectors closed in waves. Inside a combination of etched glass in window openings on the staircase landings, as well as flower stucco ornaments and vases behind the doors, have been preserved.

We now return to the corner of Bílkova and Dušní Streets, where we continue our walk. In Dušní Street stands a charming corner house no. 112/16, with balconies and a particularly interesting grille with floral motifs and stylized pottery flowers in the form of little targets on the façade. The houses on the right-hand side of the street date from 1913-1918.

At the so-called Spanish Synagogue, dating from the second half of the 19th century, we cross the small park by

A charming portal bearing masks of young girls at no. 912/6 Vězeňská Street

Osvald Polívka designed this house at no. 4 Haštalská Street, one of the most stunning Art Nouveau apartment blocks in Prague, for the builder Václav Havel

The Art Nouveau frontispieces of many apartment blocks still bear their original moral or patriotic inscriptions. This one at no. 864/13 Bílkova Street runs "Bůh žehnej práci" (God Bless Work)

These Neo-Renaissance - and Neo-Baroque-style Art Nouveau houses standing side by side on Kozí Street date from the early twentieth century. Such buildings are typical of those which line the streets of Prague

the Church of the Holy Ghost, and turn left into Vězeňská Street. House no. 912/6 from 1906, by master builder Alois Stárek, has a statue of St. Wenceslas on the upper part of the façade on the central axis. Along both sides of the windows two strikingly large architectural statues of owls are located on the same level. The St. Wenceslas inscription relates to the central statue. The front gable, with a circular window and balcony, makes the central axis longer. Above the side axes a crown bracket cornice has a false attic floor above it. Stucco ornaments - stylised bowers and wreaths - are concentrated especially round the windows and the entrance. A large stucco relief scene with birds and children adorns the centre of the façade. The portal of the house merits special attention: floral ornaments decorate the side columns. They are enclosed in a beautiful girl's head in a circle with a band.

The Art Nouveau block of flats at no. 7 is a delight. There are only small gables on the side axes above the main bracket cornice, but all the cornices in the upper part of the house, above the windows as well as above the parapets, are supported by brackets. Above the entrance into the house, sprays with fruit extend outwards from the mask of a young girl and create rich floral ornaments. Similar ornaments can be found on the façade in plenty.

However the most beautiful house, no. 914/9, dating from 1905, stands on the corner of Vězeňská and Kozí Streets. The house has a typical tower corner with a bay. The domed tower is located behind the main cornice and separates the bulky front gables situated in both streets from each other. A part of the tower under the dome, housing private appartments, gives the impression of an attic in the tower. Circular windows divide up the frontal gables. The window openings on the first and the top floors are enclosed in semi-circles. The entrances to the offices in the house are placed on a high plinth with a false bossage. Unusually rich and beautiful stucco decoration alternates with varied colourful pottery on the whole area of the façade. Most of it is concentrated on the gables, in girdles between the windows, in window half-bows and around the entrance from Kozí Street (the entrance from Vězeňská Street has not been preserved in its original form). An original lattice, formed in Art Nouveau style, protects the entrance into the house; a circular portal is ornamented with floral motifs in which ears of corn are particularly striking. The brackets under the bays, closed with threads, are interesting too. An interesting feature is that of the voluted consoles, ending in tweaks, under the bay window.

In 1900 Václav Havel built two houses at no. 4 and no.6 Haštalská Street, standing next to each other, according to a design by Osvald Polívka. They were both built in typical Art Nouveau Style. A set of central bays breaks them up vertically. House no.4 is superior to other similar houses because of its motif of a stylised tree of life which covers almost the entire frontal. It stands as one of the best examples of the most expressive features of Art Nouveau architectural decoration. The tree seems to grow from a pediment, placed above the window, under which a huge mask of a young girl is located. Sculptures of picturesque phantom-like beings are placed in gables on the side axes. The balcony grating is original, too, formed in Art Nouveau style. Both extensive features, the fully-grown tree as well as the smartness and dynamism of the curves of the metal balustrade, attest to the extraordinary imagination of the designer, architect Osvald Polívka. At the second of Havel's houses, no. 6, a corner tower wing draws our attention, as does the beautiful original decoration of the ceiling, and the circular window placed above it with a mosaic of pretty stylised flowers.

From Haštalská Street return through Kozí Street to Dlouhá Street, and directly in front of us we see corner house no.743/9, built in 1908 by the builder Janda. It is an example of a comfortable Art Nouveau tenement house with a typical front which includes a bay and is decorated with Art Nouveau vegetal motifs. Vegetal ornaments recur around the girl-like masks, in the stucco panels of the balconies and on the bay vase. Only recently the house has come to represent a kind of ideal Art Nouveau microclimate in its interior, and yet its paintings, chandeliers and elevator cages have not been preserved in their original form. Between Dlouhá and Masná Streets we notice another interesting house, no. 704/16, where an Art Nouveau floral ornament is concentrated on the front into decorations below the windows and the entrance. One cannot fail to notice the house because its corner façade bears an inscription and sign The Golden Pike.

From The Golden Pike we continue through Dlouhá Street to Hotel Paříž. However, lovers and connoisseurs of painting are recommended to turn left through Rámová Street to Haštalské Square and then onto Anežská Street, towards the St. Agnes convent complex, where a permanent exhibition of 19th century painting and sculpture is housed.

The area of the convent rates among the most precious Prague monuments, as the core of its buildings represents the first Gothic architecture in Bohemia. The whole area is, of course, worth individual inspection. We shall concentrate on the collection of painters and sculptors

This Gothic-style Art Nouveau structure, Hotel Paříž, the work of architect Jan Vejrych from 1905-1907, conjures up the image of a bow of an ocean-going steamer

whose works partly included the Art Nouveau era and who significantly influenced its artistic element. In addition to the significant works of pre-Art Nouveau artists, often influenced and instructed by their stays in Paris - Antonín Chitussi, Vojtěch Hynais and Viktor Barvitius, for example - works of painters and sculptors whose works were truly Art Nouveau in nature can be found here. For instance, the onlooker will be left entranced by the re-worked bronze group Triga by František Rous, Emanuel Hallmann and Ladislav Šaloun from 1909, located on the National Theatre building, or by the statues by Antonín Popp, Čeněk Vosmík, Josef Mauder - for example, the sculpture Fire or the design for the statue of Julius Zeyer.

For both groups of participants in the walk the starting point is the intersection of Dlouhá and Rybná Streets,

The corner façade of Hotel Paříž. Jan Köhler designed the ceramic mosaics containing folkloric and patriotic motifs

where the Art Nouveau Wohanka house no. 714, built in 1898 by architect František Buldra, is situated on the corner. The front is decorated with stucco and statues by the Art Nouveau decorator Celda Klouček.

Rybná Street leads us to Králodvorská Street, our destination. Right beside Prague's biggest department store, Kotva, we see two interesting houses. At the Neo-Gothic and Art Nouveau house no. 1085/12, elements of Art Nouveau decoration are prominent. Firstly, the portal bears vegetal ornaments and a mask of a girl's face. Stucco ornaments are enriched with architectonic sculptures of frogs around the windows, and an owl dominates the two windows on the sixth floor. A small balcony on the third floor is supported by a statue-like stylised view of the Garden of Eden. Similarly at the next Renaissance and Art Nouveau house, no. 1086/14, by architect Emil Moravec, floral

The portal of Hotel Paříž. The Art Nouveau decoration is the result of successful reconstruction

The foyer, reception desk and
staircase decoration
of Hotel Paříž

stucco decoration appears in Art Nouveau wreaths above the windows on the third floor and in bands below the narrow ledge which bears a trio of frontal gables. Stucco decorations appear on Renaissance bows on the gables.

The wide corner of Celetná and U Prašné brány Streets is made by the Art Nouveau house no. 1078/1, built in 1904 by architects Bedřich Bendelmayer, Quido Bělský and Emil Weichert. The large corner house dominates the entrance into Celetná Street and is a respectable complement to the nearby section of the Municipal House. The house has a crown ledge over its fourth floor, bearing simultaneously a balcony with wrought geometric bars along the whole house. Above the ledge an attic floor rises, elevated by a studio over the corner, completing the shallow curve of the corner. The corner bay, occupying two floors, is only a shallow one. The relatively flat front of the house is broken up by horizontal bands of rough plaster, strips of smooth plaster and an emphasised floor ledge. The stucco decoration repeats vegetal motifs below the windows and between the round corners it is enriched with reliefs of women's heads. The attic floor is embellished with colour tile decoration. Striking busts depicting women guard the entrance from the street U Prašné brány. If we walk around the house along this street we find that the next house, no. 1079/3, on the corner of the Královdvorská Street, is strikingly similar, and so they form one block of houses with an interesting glazed top section on both corners.

We have now reached our destination. In the street U Obecního domu, on the corner with Královdvorská Street, we are now standing in front of the beautiful and imposing Hotel Paříž. Construction of the hotel, the design of which was drawn up by Jan Vejrych and Antonín Pfeiffer, was begun in 1905 and completed in 1907. It is a typical Neo-Gothic building under the significant influence of Art Nouveau, as seen on the front in the stucco floral and figural decoration and also in the decorative colour-composed ceramics using an etnographic motif created by Jan Köhler.

In its time, the building provoked a wide response and because of its unique character it is presented in the Museum of Arts in Paris as an example of architecture of the Art Nouveau period. The whole building, with its Gothic high gables over the sides and the corner with a high gable and a tower at the back, resembles the bow of an ocean liner resolutely cruising the ocean waves. The corner wing offers an extensive view over the Prague roofs and church towers towards Prague Castle. The hotel has real personality, partly because of its attractive exterior and location on the edge of the ancient St. James district.

The interior of the hotel is furnished in Art Nouveau style with exceptional taste and attention to the comfort for its guests. The decoration of the hotel entrance itself is attractive, and represents an example of Art Nouveau decorative art. It surprises with its tasteful and practical use of materials, namely the high-quality floor mosaic, beautifully painted marble on the walls, elaboration of metal accessories and warm wooden panelling. The whole of the interior is wonderfully airy and light, decorated in soft harmonious colours.

The hotel offers to its visitors not only every comfort but also the atmosphere of Art Nouveau Prague as well, as evoked also by regular Thursday evening entertainment featuring the music of the first two decades of this century. A considerable advantage for visitors to Prague and hotel guests consists in the proximity of the underground, railway stations, banks, streets and the most attractive Prague historic monuments, which can be seen from the hotel windows.

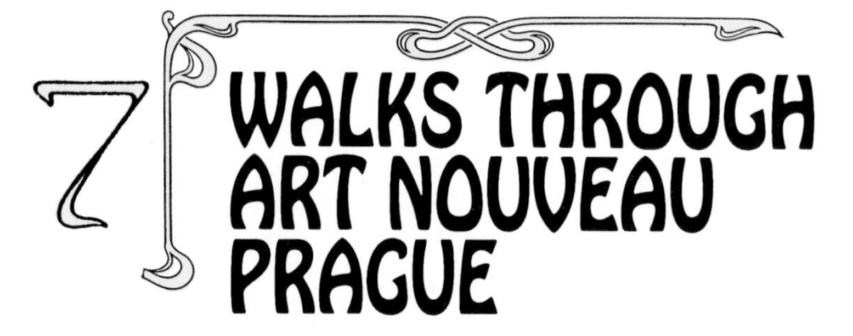

7 WALKS THROUGH ART NOUVEAU PRAGUE

An example of figural and stucco floral architectural decoration on an Art Nouveau façade. The sculptures adorn the entrance to building no. 1074/3 on Pařížská Avenue

Prague Castle aside, the Old Town Square, Pařížská Avenue (Paris Avenue) and the Jewish Town are probably the most popular tourist attractions. From Wenceslas Square we shall walk through Můstek and farther down through Melantrichova Street towards the Old Town Square. Besides the old monuments nobody can fail to see the huge statue of John Huss on the Square. Together with the monument to František Palacký it is one of the most significant Art Nouveau sculptural works. From the point of view of sculpture the beginning of the century was an which saw the creation of huge statues, encouraged by the advent of the national movement. In 1900 a tender for the best design for a monument to John Huss was announced. Sculptor Ladislav Šaloun won with his design over the renowned sculptor Stanislav Sucharda. His sketch looked like a live picture, portraying the death of John Huss at the stake,

Two Art Nouveau monuments on the Old Town Square - Šaloun's memorial to John Huss, and the Prague Municipal Fire Insurance building by Osvald Polívka

A forest of domes, roofs, towers and turrets of all shapes and sizes rises above Pařížská Avenue

Art Nouveau and Neo-Renaissance buildings on the left-hand side of Pařížská Avenue as seen from the Old Town Square

a heretic's cap on his head. He is surrounded by the victorious Hussites and suffering exiles of the era after the Battle of White Mountain. In 1903 Ladislav Šaloun presented two new sketches and was assigned the task of erecting the monument. Šaloun had realised that the substance of the statue should emphasise the values which provoked the admirer to imitate the deeds or character of the historic personality, values which would become an example for the future. The aim of the statue is to celebrate life-giving historical powers.

The main problem, however, became the location of the monument on the historic square and the related question of allowing the main figure and all figural groups, to be visible together. After several attempts Šaloun solved this problem by building a common high stone pedestal, and, moreover, by creating a relationship in movement between the groups

An Art Nouveau house (1902) at no. 1075/5 Pařížská Avenue bears the moral inscription "Staré-li seznáš, pro nové sílíš" ("He who knows the past will be stronger in the future")

around the motionless, straight figure of Huss. The historic development is expressed namely in the contrast of the rigidity of Huss's figure with the maximum relaxation of the other figures, with the motion taken to be a rotating whirl. Between the Hussites and exiles a group including a nursing mother is situated in the background, representing national enlightement, and therefore a gradual climax of masses has been expressed, creating an inclined "historical wheel" rising from the lowest place upwards again. In the stormy mass of the monument the heads of individual figures play special roles. Šaloun had created a remarkable set of heads loosely connected with the monument, having a cyclic bearing: Escape filled with resignation, Meditation and Concentration - one with eyes open and the latter with scared eyes - and finally Resignation, expressing bitterness over an unfulfilled and not understood dream. Huss himself stands above all the others, proud and straight in truth and in his belief in the future of the nation.

The foundation stone of this impressive stone and bronze group was laid in 1903 and officially unveiled on 6th July 1915 to commemorate the 500th anniversary of the burning of John Huss at the stake in Constance. Ladislav Šaloun undoubtedly reached the pinnacle of Art Nouveau art, which used above all symbols, stylisation and loose rigid shapes, and injected movement into them, which in the case of the Huss monument helped the sculptor to stress his message to the audience.

The northern side of the Old Town Square and the adjacent streets including Pařížská, were newly established and built in the area cleared during the years 1896-1899. The Prague Municipal Council had decided in 1885 on the demolition of Josefov, stretching north from the Old Town Square to the Vltava, the former Jewish town and later a refuge for the poor. The reasons stated were the high rates of mortality and illness caused by infectious diseases, a low standard of hygiene, built-up and inefficient areas, overpopulation, etc. Therefore, over subsequent years approximately 600 houses in the area earmarked for demolition were pulled down (the Jewish town originally contained over 300 houses, 31 streets, several small squares and a number of passages connecting houses and courtyards). The main axis was established in present-day Pařížská Avenue (formerly Mikulášská) 24 metres wide, which, it was expected, would become a centre of Prague social life. The streets Kaprova, Maiselova, Široká (formerly Josefovská), Břehová and Dušní were, to all intents and purposes, left in their original state, but widened. Of the old buildings only the Jewish Town Hall, six synagogues and the Old Jewish Cemetery were preserved. On the same area of the former Josefov we can now find 83 houses in 10 streets, considerably taller than the former buildings and in contrast to their diversity, creating inseparable blocks. Unfortunately, little space was set aside for green areas, except for the small park by the Old-New Synagogue.

Construction work on the cleared area started at the beginning of the 20th century on the corner of the Old Town Square. Before that the north side of the square had been enclosed by buildings, including, among others, the Art Nouveau Neo-Baroque palace of the former Prague Municipal Fire Insurance Company, at nos.932 and 934, on the basis of a design by architect Osvald Polívka a dating from 1898. The building has two sections. The left-hand, narrower one imitates the Baroque style of the demolished house, The Golden Star, at no. 932. The basement part of the house is decorated with allegorical figures of university faculties by Ladislav Šaloun on the marble panelling of the portal. The right-hand, wider part of the palace has a three-axial symmetrical front. The middle axis contains a huge niche with a lunette mosaic representing the Prague apotheosis according to a design by František Urban. Prague is represented as a female figure in rich drapery, to which burghers render homage, and in the background we see a silhouette of Prague Castle. The soft colours and the contrast of the rigid main figure with the movement of the representative of the burghers, are indicative of Art Nouveau. Allegorical groups by Bohuslav Schnirch, Extinguishing and Raising the Alarm, are situated along both sides of the mosaic concha. These statues, together with the gable, create a typical Art Nouveau configuration where centripetal force is balanced with the centrifugal. An important element is represented by the main portal, which in the upper part of the side portals bears two busts by Ladislav Šaloun representing natural elements, the female Water and the male Fire. The ecstatic expression of the faces and eyes of Fire, and the cool and cruel portrait of Water, may be considered symbols frequently used in Art Nouveau style.

With the exception of the Baroque handwriting of the author, the front of the building is an Art Nouveau work. This Art Nouveau Neo-Baroque style is based on a close combination of the smooth curves of the architecture and the statue motifs and the mosaic.

Both sides of Pařížská Avenue are now formed by uninterrupted rows of eclectic and Art Nouveau houses which create the image of a representative street with shops. A general view of Pařížská Avenue appeals to all tastes. House fronts, curved in the middle over the shops below and, crowned with a number of towers, turrets, cupolas, gables and decorative columns, evoke a feeling of beauty, luxury and accrued wealth. The attractiveness of the street is enhanced by the views of the Svatopluka Čecha Bridge, and in the opposite

A view up the centre of a spiral staircase at house no. 125/16, U Dvou Malorusek (The Two Little Russian Girls). The picture shows a stylistically shaped banister with lattice work

A peacock is perched on the top of a bay window protruding from the Renaissance-style Art Nouveau building at no. 981/17 Pařížská Avenue

direction by the Old Town Square with the Town Hall tower and the towers of The Church of St. Gall in the background.

Let us now walk along this boulevard and enjoy its architectonic beauty. We stop first of all at the beginning of the street. On the right-hand side, towards the crossroads with Široká Street, we see a block of houses built in the historicising styles of the Neo-Renaissance and the Neo-Baroque. The very beginning of the left-hand side of Pařížská Avenue offers us a piece of Art Nouveau beauty. House no 1073/1, connected to the Church of St. Nicholas, although a Neo-Baroque building, is interesting in many aspects. It was built (1902) on the site of a former monastery by architect Jan Koula, owner of the house. "With a strong will towards the set aim", the inscription on house no. 1074/3 states, and the statue of a woman with a crown, shield and banner expresses such determination. From an architectonic point of view the building represents a kind of transition, being a combination of Neo-Baroque and Art Nouveau styles, built by architect Rudolf Koukol in 1901-1902. An important feature is that of the two statues of female figures below the bays, symbolically representing human activities. The Art Nouveau style of house no. 1075/5, built in 1902, is given by the name of its builder and architect, Matěj Blecha. The three-axial house has on its central axis a huge two-storey bay with double windows, completed with a balcony. Decorations are formed by horizontal and vertical sculptured stucco bands with vegetal ornaments. The decorations on the side axes are the most expressive, taking the form of a vase from which branches with ribbons grow, and below which two figures hold wreaths. Above the entrance we see a beautiful girl, and in the upper corners the portal groups, four child-

This statue of Rabbi Loew by Ladislav Šaloun stands at the corner of the New Town Hall façade on Mariánské Square

This bronze statue of Moses by František Bílek
is a feature of the park at the
Old-New Synagogue

An evening shot across the Svatopluka Čecha Bridge
to the lights of Prague Castle and
the Hanava Pavilion

ren's heads, are situated. The front gable bears in its corners large hedlike statues. In the centre of the bay we may read - as on other houses in this street - a moral inscription, "Having learnt the old, one strives for the new".

Two other houses, nos. 1076/7 and 68/9, were designed in 1902-1904 by architect Jan Vejrych. Their substance and decoration are not Art Nouveau in style, but Art Nouveau influenced them by means of decorative elements, which seem to be modelled strictly, rigidly and heavily. House no. 68/9, owned by the commercial company Merkur, is particularly interesting. Its corner bears a bust of the opera singer Otakar Mařák by sculptor Jan Kavan and architect Bedřich Hanák. The reliefs of the continents were created by Antonín Popp. The side of the house in Jáchymova Street is striking, especially because of its rich Baroque gable completed by a sculpture. This building is followed by another Art Nouveau house, no. 67/11, built in 1902 by Antonín Makovec. The front has standard, strictly repetitive stucco decorations formed by minor Art Nouveau floral ornaments in semicircles over the windows and in mezzanines in the window axes. The wrought bars of the entrance are equally beautiful. At the same time, however, architect Jan Vejrych built the next house, no. 66/13, in Neo-Renaissance style. House no. 15, built by Matěj Blecha in 1906, is a huge, expressively Neo-Gothic house with Art Nouveau elements on its frontal. The most interesting element on the corner of the house is an Art Nouveau sculpture of St.George and the dragon. The coats of arms are Neo-Gothic decoration as well. A spacious house at no. 981/17, which forms a corner by the Old-New Synagogue in the Jewish Town, was designed by architects Richard Klenka of Vlastimil and František Weyr in 1906. It is an abundantly articulated house in the Neo-Renaissance and Art Nouveau styles, one of the most prominent in this part of Pařížská Avenue. The central section of the huge tower corner bears remarkable arcades, and the slightly convex bay over Pařížská Avenue is panelled with dark wood with carved decorations and colour paintings. Perhaps the most beautiful element is a carved peacock with a golden crown situated in the upper part of the bay. The house has an entrance from Pařížská Avenue, formed by a hall entrance, the ceiling of which is painted similarly to the bay, and an excellently crafted grating consisting of spirals with leaves. At the sides of the entrance sculptured vases with fruit are situated in niches. The artistic work of the old artisans can be admired in the balcony grating on the façade, as well as in the grating protecting the window ledges. The paintings of the bay are repeated in the plaster above and below the windows, which are stressed even more by drawn-out window ledges. In the basement of the house there is a stylish restaurant, At The Old Synagogue.

The right-hand row of houses from the corner of Pařížská Avenue and Široká Street to the next corner, where Pařížská and Bílkova Streets meet, is most interesting. While on the

The bronze decoration of the bridge railings containing dolphins and the personification of Prague, with below it a sculpted wrought relief designed by Karel Klusáček. The bronze statue of a torch-bearer stands on one of the bridge's piers overlooking the river

This interesting shot of Pařížská and Maiselova Streets running in parallel shows early - 20th century houses and the historic buildings of the Jewish Quarter, namely the Old-New Synagogue and the Town Hall

An exquistely decorated portal of the Neo-Baroque Art Nouveau building at no. 96/9 Široká Street with its expressive figural statues

houses at either end of this row Art Nouveau façades prevail, the five houses in the middle of the row are built rather in Neo-Renaissance style, albeit with Art Nouveau decorative elements. The whole row of houses, especially its middle section, seems to protrude over Pařížská Avenue with its bays and gables. The corner house, U Dvou Malorusek, at no. 125/16, was built by Matěj Blecha in 1906. The house is dominated by two large corner sculptures of maidens carrying fruit. The corner is bossed, and individual bosses are scattered all over the façade as well. The house has a preserved original staircase with an Art Nouveau banister grating, mosaic mezzanine windows and the additional, equally remarkable features. Other houses in this row were built by the famous architects Karel Mašek, Emanuel Dvořák and Jan Vejrych in approximately 1906. The houses are definitely similar in terms of the type of architectonic treatment given to the frontispieces. All the houses have huge angular double bays, between which balconies and loggias with various figural sculptures are situated, and have rich stucco decorations and articulated gables. House no. 126/18 has an attractive original metal grating and entrance hall, and under the main ledge are rich ornamental decorations with masks and figural reliefs - a night watchman with a halberd and a horn, and two female figures. At house no. 127/20 we notice first of all the sculptures of mythical birds below the window ledges on the third floor and over the entrance. A huge interesting bay becomes an arcade in its upper part. In addition to the interesting floral decorations inside the house there is a beautiful wrought-iron elevator cage. Also at the next house, no. 128/22, U Dvořáků, it is the birds which immediately catch the eye. They sit with their wings spread over the balcony columns. Especially in the case of this house, we may note how all the Art Nouveau architectonic figural and animal sculptures project systematically outwards towards the viewer. Houses no. 129/24 and 130/26 have more sober stucco floral elements, pleasant masks of young girls and a typically Art Nouveau-style stucco technique. The end of the row of houses on the right-hand side is formed by corner house no. 131/28, situated in Bílkova Street as well. Its composition is totally different in comparison with the preceding houses, that its gable, corners and decorations are dissimilar. A convex bay is situated on the central front axis. Below the next corner bay window, Art Nouveau style is represented especially by two beautiful stucco peacocks with crowns. The corner has no tower or striking gable. There is an elevated attic, on the corners of which are very slim vases, making the building optically higher when viewed. The entire house façade is divided by ledges over the windows and stucco bands with floral motifs. Its appearance is enlivened by the wrought-iron

An example of beautiful Art Nouveau decoration in the entrance hall of no. 96/9 Široká Street

grating, stucco, and the coloured, glazed, ceramic, ornamental mosaics and intricate portraits which seem to be scattered all over the frontal surface. As in the case of the majority of the houses, bosses appear on the elevated shop basement. Above the monumental entrance two child sculptures support the bay, holding a big loose wreath. Immediately over the house entrance an inscription saying "Built MCMVI A.D. Architect Mašek" is set in a decorative oval. In the interior pretty mosaic tiles with tiny ornaments have been preserved, and windows with coloured glass can be seen on the staircase landing; however, the most beautiful elements are the appartment doors, over which a lovely mask of a young girl is set on a carved column.

In the only little park by the Old-New Synagogue, a sculpture of Moses by František Bílek of 1905 is situated. On this left-hand side of Pařížská Avenue the corner house U První reduty, no. 19, built in Neo-Baroque style, is worth seeing. The neighbouring house, no. 21, appears to be Neo-Renaissance in style, however it is rather similar to the nextdoor Art Nouveau house, no. 205/23. House no. 21 was built by Čeněk Křička in 1905. On the middle axis the division of the frontal is concentrated, with a pointed roofed bay resembling a tower, and on the second floor a brick balcony runs out asymetrically from the bay. On the second floor a wide balcony with wrought bars with geometrical patterns is situated. Architects Antonín Makovec and Jiří Justich built Art Nouveau house no. 205/23 in 1905-1906. This three-axial house has on the side axes slightly convex closed bays, emphasized with metal panels. The elevated bossed shop basement is extended by sculptured plaster on the second floor. The central axis of the house, on which a huge abstract sculpture in the middle and a small brick balcony on the fifth floor are situated, moves fluently into a high, sober gable with a window and two smaller round windows. The stucco decoration of the gable is represented by two connected wreathes.

In addition to stucco decoration, the façade was enriched with ceramics. A splendid colour ceramic with floral ornaments fills in the sectors over the windows and semi-circles on the second floor, and the entire entrance to the house is faced with tiles. Sculptured coloured ceramic columns on both sides of the entrance create a beautiful and unusual decoration.

At the end of Pařížská Avenue we come to the first and only purely Art Nouveau Prague bridge built in iron, originally called New Bridge in Asanační Street, now called Svatopluka Čecha Bridge. The bridge should have been a continuation of a new major modern city street, namely a boulevard starting at Wenceslas Square and continuing through Můstek, the Old Town Square to the new Asanační Street, then along the bridge and upwards through a cutting or a tunnel to Letná, and further still to the newly-built city quarter, Bubeneč. With the exception of the construction of a new street from the Old Town Square to the planned bridge, the original intention was, fortunately, not realized; though the plan for a bridge was retained, a fully adequate way of extending the road to Letná was not found.

The new bridge in Asanační (Pařížská) Street was the last project to be implemented and accepted without a public tender. At the time the bridge department of the building office drew up the construction design, view and the architectonic design was entrusted to the architect Jan Koula. The bridge project was completed by the bridge department in 1904 and accepted in June 1905. The supports and pillars were built by the Müller and Kapsa company and the iron construction of the vaults was supplied and mounted by three Prague bridge works, each vault by a different company: that on the right bank hy the Prášil brothers; the central vault by Prague Machine Works Ltd.; and that on the left bank by the Bohemian and Moravian Machine Factory in Prague. All the pillars were completed in April 1907, and of the final stonelaid in the presence of Emperor Franz Josef I and the Archbishop of Prague. The bridge was opened to the public in June 1908. Its artistic decoration exceeded that of all other modern bridges, and although not everything has been preserved it remains a magnificent example of Art Nouveau influence on this type of purpose-made structure. The most dominant elements are the bronze statues of the four Victorias, two at each end of the bridge. The Victorias are over three metres high and hold gilded sprigs. Each of them standson top of a cast-iron column 17.5 metres high. Originally they stood at both ends facing the bridge, but during repair work carried out in the 1950s they were turned to face the bridge entrances. The cast-iron statues were made by the sculptor Antonín Popp. The entrance pillars were abundantly decorated as well. The heads facing upstream have statues of torch-bearers by sculptors Ludvík Herzl and Karel Opatrný, whilst the heads facing downstream bear six-headed bronze hydras with the Prague coat of arms by sculptor Ludvík Wurzel. Moreover, the pillars are decorated with bronze and granite festoons, and bronze statues also decorate the front bridge bows - chiselled bronze fillings with dolphins and lockets and a personification of Prague by Ludvík Wurzel.The upper parts of the bridge are covered with fillings made of copper plates with motifs of waves designed by Karel Klusáček.

The bridge decoration included night illumination, flower baskets on the polls and bronze vases on the stone balus-

A colourful ceramic representation of Madonna and Child at house no. 96/9 on the corner of Maiselova and Široká Streets

trades of the entrance pillars. The decorative bridge elements were, however, partly taken away and deposited because of frequent attempts to steal their precious, beautifully crafted metals, and also because of possible damage during the war.

The official opening of the bridge in June 1908 was at the same time connected with giving the bridge a name in commemoration of the popular writer and poet Svatopluk Čech. The bridge is used also at present, under heavy traffic. The Old Town bridgehead offers us a beautiful view of Prague Castle, Strahov monastery and Petřín hill, as well as of the Hanava Pavilion across the river. Views from Letná of the bridge and Pařížská Avenue and the Old Town Square in the background, are equally beautiful.

From Čech bridge we walk along Dvořákovo nábřeží to enjoy the views of the river and then we turn down Na Rejdišti, which leads to 17.listopadu Street at the Museum of Applied Art. We recommend a visit to the museum to everybody who is interested in applied art during various eras and styles, and of course, there is a world-famous collection from the Art Nouveau period. The large building itself was built during 1897-1901 on a design by Josef Schulz in French Neo-Renaissance style. The reliefs of crafts on the front were created by Bohuslav Schnirch and Antonín Popp. On the elevated ground floor we find exhibition halls and a specialist public library, founded back in 1888, now including about one hundred volumes, publications and magazines concerning the history of art and sculpture. The museum collection includes developmental lines of various branches of arts and crafts, from ancient times to the present day. The collection of glass exhibits is world famous. The huge wall paintings which we can see between the second and third floors represent allegories of various craft branches and are the work of Ferdinand Herčík.

After a visit to the museum we return only a few dozen metres along the wall of the Jewish Cemetery, turn left down Břehová Street and continue our Art Nouveau walk. Just beside the corner Neo-Baroque tenement house we find Art Nouveau house no. 209/6, built in approximately 1909 by V. Pickl and Václav Vejrych. The house has a typical three-axial composition with two slightly convex bays in the central part and balconies on the side axes. The front and the balcony bars on the side axes are decorated with large metallic oval elements. Statuettes of owls are situated below the main ledge and abstract architectonic statues of insects are located below the bays. The flat rough plaster in the upper part of the house is interrupted by geometric ornaments. The opposite building no. 43/3, located in the Old Jewish Cemetery wall, differs from the other houses in its modernist style. It was built as a family house in 1913-1915 by architect Antonín Engel, who also created the huge block of houses dated 1910-1911, nos. 4-8, with a figural sculpture in the corner niche.

A few dozens metres farther on at the corner of Břehová and Maiselova Streets, we find the large late Art Nouveau house no. 41/21. Its frontal faces onto Maiselova Street and it stands out among the other houses with its decorations. The step-like image of the huge house is created namely by the central rizalit and the side bay. A step-like central gable with a round window decorated with statues of vases is situated above the attic. The entire frontal is covered with regular green and gilded geometric ornaments in squares. In some of them, especially at the sides of the middle bay, we can see silhouettes of heads of various personalities of the Jewish community, and the Star of David. Two more figural reliefs are seen in the upper part of the house. The decoration reflects the interest in the Empire and Biedermeier styles typical of that period. This is evident also from the style of the two big statues of women seated with flowers on both sides of the entrance. The house was built by František Weyr and Richard Klenka of Vlastimil in 1911 as one of the first luxury tenement houses in Prague.

Other houses in the row towards the intersection with Široká ulice have been affected by the Art Nouveau period evidently only very slightly. They have sober fronts, the purposeful decoration of which is acquired by a combination of rough and smooth plaster and geometric ornaments appear only in horizontal or vertical bands. An interesting detail can be found for example at house no. 42/19, where on the frontal broken only by slightly convex bays, the bodies of wasps or bees form in swarms below the upper and main ledges. The house has been made to fit in with the neighbouring buildings by means of an attic floor, the front of which has been decorated with geometric tile shapes. The front of the next house, no. 39/17, built in 1910-1912 by František Troníček and Josef Čácha, is decorated only with plain bays and geometric shapes in rough plaster, and the neighbouring house no. 38/15 by Josef Vajshajtl, built in 1910-1912, has a remarkable figural relief inspired most probably by ancient Egypt. At the intersection of Maiselova and Široká Streets, after we pass the Jewish Town Hall, we see two beautiful Art Nouveau houses, the corners of which face each other. House no. 96/9 has a splendid entrance, emphasized especially by two big figural sculptures and the sculpture of an owl between them. The front bears round ceramic mosaic pictures of monarchs, and right on the corner there is a picture of the Madonna and Child. The vast area behind the door contains marble panels, a floor mosaic and stucco decoration. The windows on the staircase landings have mo-

No. 15/11 Kaprova Street: the glazed, ceramic, stylized, above life-size figure of a woman dates from around 1910 and is the work of Richard Luksch

saic glass panelling. This magnificent house was built by Karel Vítězslav Mašek in 1908.

From its intersection with Široká Street as far as Kaprova Street, Maiselova Street offers us an exhibition of articulated, imposing, nearly over-decorated tenement houses of various styles, with many gables of various shapes and a variety of towers and turrets, the largest of which is the corner tower of house no. 56/10 from 1907, with an Art Nouveau façade. Over the corner bay we again find peacocks and at the top on the corner axis a round window panelled with a coloured glass mosaic. The stucco decoration repeatedly uses, in particular, wreaths and figural reliefs with inscriptions. An Art Nouveau frontal can be found also among the beautiful eclectic houses in Maiselova Street, on house no. 5, and especially on house no. 60/3, where the bossing over the portal stands out, and between the window on the second floor and over the entrance we see the prominent mask of a girl and stucco branches with leaves. We have now passed the Maisel Synagogue on the left, and on the right-hand side we turn into Kaprova Street. The decoration on house no. 15/11, built by František Pohl and Leopold Neugebauer in 1906-1907, is worth seeing. The architects used the effect of coloured ceramic decoration: in a band (like a braid) composed of conventionalised black, white and gold leaves, as well as between the windows on the second and top floors, where the floral pictures are composed of ceramics. In this environment two above life-size glazed ceramic figures stand out. These decorative compositions were created for this house in Kaprova Street in approximately 1910 by sculptor Richard Luksch, a member of Klimt's Viennese Art Nouveau group. The composition is motivated by a fashionable theme of a priestess facing the street and invoking with raised hands superhuman, divine and natural powers. This was a very popular figure which expressed the mythological orientation of the Art Nouveau imagination. The long figure, represented in geometric, ornamental shapes, shows its ability to embody symbolically also invisible and superhuman elements. On the opposite side of the street, on house no. 52/6, another abstract shape - a wasp motif - shows the frequent Art Nouveau inspiration drawn from nature. The motif recurs in the grating door, over the entrance and at the sides in ceramics, plaster and stucco. The design of this tenement house with shops, built in 1906-1908, was made by the famous architect Bedřich Bendelmayer.

In Žatecká Street we should mention the huge plastic decoration of the gables of Art Nouveau house no. 53/10 by architects Václav Vejrych and V. Pickl from 1909-1910. An example of a Neo-Gothic Art Nouveau front can be seen in the neighbouring houses nos. 54/12 and 14: sculptured Gothic pointed arches filled with rich floral stucco decoration.

Before we proceed from Kaprova Street to Valentinská Street we should note corner house no. 57/9 with a cupola. In Valentinská Street we can admire the coloured ceramic decoration on the frontals of houses nos. 20/10 and 22/12, to which the interior decoration corresponds. The Art Nouveau layout of the houses indicates that this is the work of an experienced architect - again Bedřich Bendelmayer.

Coming to the main street, 17. listopadu Street, and continuing a little farther to the left, on the corner of Platnéřská Street we find the entire complex of the Convent of the Knights of the Cross at no. 181/4, the construction of which was completed by Josef Sakař in 1909-1913. It is an example of beautiful Neoclassical Art Nouveau, in terms of both the structure of the buildings and the sober decoration of the frontal and the pompous main entrance, including the ubiquitous Art Nouveau wreath accompanied by decorative sculptured vases.

We now complete our walk in Kaprova Street and return to Wenceslas Square on the A-line of the underground. However, we recommend an inspection of the sculptured decoration on the building of the modern Town Hall at Mariánské náměstí no. 2, reached by walking down Platnéřská Street. The modern Town Hall is a vast complex between Mariánské and Malé Squares, built in 1908-1911 on a design by architect Osvald Polívka. It was an official building, and therefore the architect had to accept some intervention on the part of the institution making the request, the Provincial Commitee. Osvald Polívka used his experience of the Art Nouveau period, but its development during construction was impaired by regressive Baroque-like elements. This fact is the main reason for the lack of modern architectonic expression in the building. The modern Town Hall stands out rather for its original sculptural decoration by significant Czech sculptors. In the hall of the building we find a figural relief by Antonín Štrunc. The front bears allegorical reliefs lining a monumental staircase. The upper section containe the allegorical groups, Auditing and Accounting, by Stanislav Sucharda, on the balcony, and on the eaves on the left-hand side the groups eantitled Modesty, Nobility, Power and Perseverance by Josef Mařatka. The sculptures Iron Man and Rabbi Löw, by Ladislav Šaloun, stand separately in the corners of the frontal. In this way we can finish our walk just as we started it - with a commemoration of the work of the Art Nouveau sculptor, Ladislav Šaloun.

This impressive shot of one part of the Old Town Square shows the Art Nouveau monument (by sculptor Ladislav Šaloun) to John Huss in the foreground

The portal of the stunning Art Nouveau house (Gorazdova Street) at no. 1996/13, erected between 1903 and 1905, is adorned with a bust representing a young woman in the window opening above the door. The stucco decoration displaying floral motifs is also worthy of note

8 WALKS THROUGH ART NOUVEAU PRAGUE

There is a very good reason for stopping for a while right at the beginning of this tour and having a look at the magnificent building no. 699/30 (Vodičkova Street), U Nováků, built at the beginning of the century. The structure was designed in 1902-1903 by Osvald Polívka to serve as a department store. Osvald Polívka is certainly one of the most important personalities of Czech Art Nouveau architecture, and we shall have many more opportunities to admire his work during the present walk through the streets of Prague. Many of his designs belong to the finest examples of Czech Art Nouveau architecture. Others - such as Zemská banka Na Příkopě, Hasičská pojišťovna (the Fire Insurance building) on the Old Town Square, or the interiors of the Municipal House - display many Neo-Baroque and eclectic elements. On the other hand still more, for instance U Nováků, the Czech Insurance Company, building which stands beside

Topič Publishing House on National Avenue - or several of his residential buildings - represent pure Art Nouveau architecture par excellence. Much can be said about the decorative side of Osvald Polívka's creations. It is known that the decorations were either created by Polívka himself, or that prominent artists of the time were invited to cooperate, namely Mucha, Mařatka, Sucharda or Preisler. Jan Preisler was the author of the decorations on the U Nováků building. The beautiful stucco decorations by Polívka bear the hallmark both of his outstanding talent for drawing and of his boundless imagination. The façades of Polívka's buildings are often decorated with stucco work depicting fantastic creatures from the world of fairy tales and folk legends. The façade of the U Nováků building on Vodičkova Street is an excellent example of this.

The U Nováků building was a very modern structure indeed. It contained a split-level sales area that, despite being

Practically every element of Art Nouveau decoration can be found on the magnificently bedecked façade of the famous Art Nouveau house U Nováků from 1903

much smaller, reminded the visitor of the Parisian department stores of the time. The basic structure of the building is symmetrical and the entire Art Nouveau decoration is composed of metal, wrought-iron, glass, painting and stucco elements. The building has a wide frontispiece with shorter lateral axes on the second floor bearing two horn-shaped oriels with balconies at their tops. The entire central section of the second floor of the building is adorned by a wide balcony. The building is made to appear taller by the applied imitation of vertical bossed strips. Over the conspicuously protruding cornice in the centre rises the topmost attic floor with its generously glazed central portion. The lateral axes of the building are crowned with masonry gables decorated by basrelief vases in the columns. The first two floors, containing large windows, represent the commercial part of the building with the marble rendering of the façade. The signpost U Nováků under the balcony is written in Art Nouveau script. The viewer will probably be most impressed by the colourful and rich decoration of the façade. Its entire centre is covered with allegorical paintings representing Commerce (Obchod) and Industry (Průmysl). The paintings were based on Jan Preisler's cartoon sketches, with the addition of some folklore attributes popular at the time. The elegance and beauty of the elaborate wrought-iron balustrades decorating the balconies of the building evoke the sensation of plasticity and motion. Above the windows and under the cornice, as well as above and below the oriels, there are many ornamental frescos with floral motifs. Polívka's sculptured frogs, and especially the frog-queens around the oriels, constitute extremely charming decorative elements. The entire ornamentation is sup-

Two decorative Art Nouveau elements on the façade of the house U Nováků - a stucco head on the oriel and the well-executed design of a small frog

plemented by stucco medallions in the shape of female breasts located around the lateral oriels. Above the windows of the smaller balconies the year 1903 can be read. To make the impression of the building complete, the sides of the lower part of the oriel are adorned by two gold-crested pheasants. The façade strives to achieve the impression of city elegance, and thus the rich colouring of the exterior is calmed by the extensive usage of gilded decorative elements.

Further down Vodičkova Street stands an interesting residential Art Nouveau building, no. 682/20, built by Mr. F. Buldra. Mr. Buldra, a civil engineering contractor by profession, prepared the design of the building in question himself. White decoration is applied to the background of the light green façade of the building. The two floors of the building are visually connected by a moderately protruding rectangular oriel with columns and a balcony at the top. The main protruding fillet, supported by cantilevers, in turn supports the masonry attic balustrade with stucco floral ornaments. Surprisingly enough, the front gable is low and not very large. On the other hand, the floor fillets are very robust and visually almost overhanging. The façade is interesting thanks to the presence of many rich Art Nouveau decorative elements, such as the masks of girls' faces located between the windows, and under the window parapet fillets supplemented by many floral stucco ornaments. The decorative impression of the frontal view of the building is enhanced by the presence of two figural sculptures standing on the fillet above the entrance gate.

Leaving Buldra's house behind, we approach the tower of the New Town Municipal Council building. On the left-hand side we pass Řeznická Street, where at the corner of

The allegorical paintings Obchod (Commerce) and Průmysl (Industry) in the centre of the frontispiece of the house U Nováků were created on the basic of a design by the painter Jan Preisler

house no. 672 a commemorative plaque by František Bílek states that on this site once stood the house where Jerome of Prague was born in 1365. He was burned at the stake after being found guilty of heresy by the Council of Constance in 1416. Just here, on this side of Charles Square (Karlovo náměstí), we face the lively green and yellow decorated façade of Art Nouveau house no. 559/28.

It is worth stopping for a while to have a look around the largest square in Prague, originally founded to serve as a cattle market. The most interesting building on Charles Square is the Gothic-Renaissance Municipality Building dating from the 14th-16th centuries. Next to the old council building is the Neoclassical structure erected at the beginning of this century. Another dominant structure of the square is the Baroque building of the Church of St. Ignatius and the adjacent complex of Jesuit monastery buildings stretching to the south and

The façade of the Art Nouveau building at no. 1995/11 Gorazdova Street, dating from 1907, is dotted with bay windows, eaves and sculptures

occupying the whole eastern section of the square. Another important structure is the Neo-Renaissance building located on the lower part of the square, belonging to Prague Polytechnic. The area of Charles Square is reached by two main arteries, namely Ječná Street and Žitná Street. Leaving the square to the south is the street connecting Charles Square with Vyšehrad. After enjoying a stroll through the park area of the square with its many memorials and sculptures, we shall pass along Resslova and Václavská Streets to Trojanova Street, where our tour of Prague Art Nouveau treasures continues.

In Trojanova Street our attention is immediately drawn to the huge yellow and green building, no. 339/13. It is a late Art Nouveau structure, built in 1912 to serve as a school building. The original purpose of the structure and its general impression correspond to one another. The architect, František

This wide painted gable on Art Nouveau house (Gorazdova Street) no. 1996/13, culminating in manificent stucco branches, is one of the most beautiful to grace the streets of Prague

Schlaffer, designed the frontal of the building as a rather sober, yet imposing, structure. This effect is accomplished chiefly by a huge portal with sandstone columns. The only decorations to be found here are the standard stucco green wreaths and festoons contrasting with the yellow background of the plaster. The frontal aspect of the building is crowned with wreath-decorated gables. Directly opposite the school stands residential building no. 343/16, dating from 1905, identifiable by its white stucco Art Nouveau decorations, i. e. wreaths and ribbons on the darker background colour of the façade.

From Trojanova Street we continue to Dittrichova Street, where several interesting houses with Art Nouveau façades can be found. The most striking structure is apartment building no. 2024/5, with its oriel located on a central axis and displaying pure Art Nouveau decorations. The façade is visually broken up by patterns of different colours.

Art Nouveau and classical elements are present in the decoration of the façade of the First Czech Mutual Benefit Insurance Company building at no. 76/14 Spálená Street, constructed on a design by Osvald Polívka in 1907

The short and inconspicuous Gorazdova Street, running parallel to Dittrichova, is home to several remarkable buildings. For example, house no. 1995/11 is a pure Art Nouveau structure, the curved eaves having been built in 1907 by architect Jan Petrák. The decoration of the façade comprises not only the figural basrelief and wrought-iron grilles of the balconies and the usual ornamental stucco bands, but also the upper oriels covered with dark tiles and the patterns formed by smooth and rough surface plaster. Still richer and more diverse decorations can be found on the façade of house no. 1996/13, called U Kapínů. The grand impression is given by depicting the scene of a female figure holding a lyre and a crowd of ordinary onlookers against the background of Prague Castle. Such compositions must have been very popular during the period of exuberant nationalism which preceded the First World War. The gable of the building is decorated at the top by a huge

An Art Nouveau relief on the lunette located on the side gable of the First Czech Mutual Benefit Insurance Comapany in Spálená Street

Architect Osvald Polívka designed these Art Nouveau buildings on Národní Avenue, once home to the Prague Insurance Company and the Topič publishing house

stucco tree. However, the visitor to the street will probably notice first of all the rich portal decoration bearing a bust and the original carved wooden doors. The Art Nouveau decoration can be seen also on several other houses in Gorazdova Street; of these the Renaissance-Art Nouveau house at no. 1997/15 is worth mentioning.

Leaving Gorazdova Street and crossing Jiráskovo Square we enter Náplavní Street. Here we find two Art Nouveau buildings built by Josef Hercík in 1907, namely houses no. 2011/5 and no. 2012/3. The façade of the former is beautifully decorated by a colourful mosaic on the gable above the main cornice. The stucco decorations are arranged to form horizontal and vertical bands. The neighbouring houses no. 2009/9 and no. 2010/7 in Náplavní Street are two identical Art Nouveau buildings with rich decoration, represented chiefly by the masks under the cornice. The façade is visually broken up by two huge polygonal oriels resting on wall brackets. Under the oriels are located massive masonry balconies with decorative floral motifs. The colouring is accomplished using simple green tiles on the gables and oriels. The houses are provided with hanging eaves supported by small brackets. The entrance gates are decorated by pillars, whose capitals are adorned with vases and flowers. Both the entrance gate and the interior windows are adorned with a beautiful coloured mosaic designed to form a floral motif. Building no. 2020/4 towers over the corner of Náplavní and Myslíkova Streets. The corner oriel is decorated with floral ornaments and the sides of the building are visually broken up by balconies with ornamental wrought-iron grilles. Opposite Náplavní Street, in Myslíkova Street proper, stands the interesting building named U Kheilů with a wide main gable and overhanging cornice. The sober Art Nouveau façade is divided by windowsills and decorated with Art Nouveau wreaths. At the end of Myslíkova Street, another object of interest can be found, namely house no. 284 standing on the corner with Charles Square. The building was built by Osvald Polívka in 1905. Above the corner oriel, on the third and fourth floors, is a comparatively small gable; the gables facing Myslíkova Street are also rather small and inconspicuous. The whole visual structure of the house is asymmetrical: the façade facing Myslíkova Street is rather dull, with no decoration present. On the other hand, the façade facing Charles Square is symmetrically divided by two protruding oriels with small gables above. The visual division of the façade is enhanced by the imitation bossing on the second floor. The additional decorative attributes of the Neo-Baroque Art Nouveau can be seen in the amount of stucco work depicting stylized sea shells. All the stucco decorations are concentrated on the gable and the corner façade above the windows. The decoration on the gable takes the form of a huge stucco wreath, and on the top floor situated between the windows is a figural composition representing the Assumption of the Virgin Mary. The author of the composition is probably Antonín Sucharda. Right in the centre of the corner façade an imitation sundial can be seen.

Turning to the left we proceed into Spálená Street. Right behind the church stands the building of the First Czech Mutual Insurance Corporation, bearing the number 76/14. The 1907 design by Osvald Polívka indicates the advent of classicism. The classicist influence in the design can be perceived in the decoration centred around the oriels and at the sides of the gable, in the bands of rustic motifs, and the vases located on the lower side of the cornice. On the other hand, the preceding period of Art Nouveau manifests itself in stucco basrelief on the bright blue background in oblong fields above the first floor and in the arches of the lateral gables. The façade therefore bears the marks of both the Art Nouveau and classicist styles. The same may be said of the entrance hall. Here the decoration is dominated by beautiful coloured windows and a mosaic on the rear wall of the water fountain. The author of the mosaic was Jan Kryšpín. The magnificence of the hall is emphasized by the staircase, whose balustrade is decorated with unusual stylized figures. Opposite the department store in Spálená Street there is another interesting building designed by Osvald Polívka in 1905. This house, no. 112/55, is considered to represent the Baroque paraphrase of the Art Nouveau style as conceived by Polívka's talent and intellect. The structural bearing and vertical impression of the façade divided by a centrally positioned oriel with two lateral gables, bears a resemblance to the Peterka Building on Wenceslas Square designed by Jan Kotěra. The façade decoration is dominated by huge masks of young girls staring down from the window niche. The viewer will also be captivated by the very elaborate wrought-iron grille on the balcony balustrade with its floral ornamental motifs and beautiful wrought-iron entrance grille. Osvald Polívka allowed himself to be inspired by the fairy tale world, this time in the stucco figures of horned devils. On entering the corridor of the house one sees the commemorative plaque reading "Here lived, and fought through his creative work for modern Czech art, the sculptor Otto Gutfreund, from 1889 to 1927".

Passing between the department store and the underground station we approach building no. 1978/26 (was built in 1902) in Vladislavova Street, which also bears the hallmarks of its allegiance to the Art Nouveau era, mainly in the style of its stucco decorations on the oriel and around the windows. The frontal gable features a charming stucco swan. However, a far more interesting, and artistically more valuable building stands around the corner in Jungmannova Street. House no. 748/30 was built in 1911-1913 on a design by Jan Kotěra for the publisher of musical literature and scores, Mojmír Urbánek. The building includes the concert hall called the Mozarteum (hence the reason why this house is known by the same name). The optical sculptural nature of the frontispiece of the house is accomplished through the use of different kinds of masonry (mostly brickwork). The ground floor of the façade is decorated by a pair of female figures sculptured by Jan Štursa. The house is not built in Art Nouveau style; it belongs to the so-called modern style. On the opposite side of the street is house no. 25/15, known as the Beaufort Publishing House, built in 1908-1909 on a design by Osvald Polívka. The visual division of the façade is accomplished by two polygonal oriels, the lower parts of which are interconnected by a balcony. The two wall paintings (portraits of Jiří Melantrich and

Karel Starší of Žerotín) were placed by the architect between the windows on the second floor. In the lateral axes of the façade above the second floor windows two stucco suprafenestras can be seen, depicting The Telegraph and The Telephone, allegories by an unknown stucco author.

Art Nouveau architecture in Prague pervaded many places, including sacred buildings. Kamil Hilbert, the architect who completed the construction of Saint Vitus' Cathedral at Prague Castle, and the author, among other things, of the beautiful Gothic-Renaissance building at Masarykovo nábřeží, is the man whom we have to thank for returning the Church of Saint Martin in the Wall to its original purpose. The church is of great historic value because it was here that in 1414 the first mass according to the reformed Hussite rites was celebrated.

A detail from the decoration on the former home to the Prague Insurance Company, showing a colourful floral ceramic mosaic under the eaves of the building, and two statues of owls on the corners of the balcony

Ladislav Šaloun created the figural reliefs on the façade of the former insurance building on National Avenue

The Art Nouveau building erected for the Topič publishing house. A wonderful figural mosaic sits in the circular niche above the window

This part of the bronze sculptural group called Triga on the National Theatre building, dating from 1910-1911, shows horses rearing up

The church is located in Martinská Street. The Art Nouveau ideas in the interpretation of Kamil Hilbert found their way into the reconstruction of the church building in 1905. The very difficult task of sensitive reconstruction confined Art Nouveau elements in the main to small details. On this site the meeting of the two modern concepts of the time took place: the ancient building, entirely preserved to the present day, was reconstructed accurately, and the missing structures were supplemented with modern creations, accentuating the artistic impression of the finished work. The Art Nouveau elements in the Church of Saint Martin in the Wall can be found in the de tails of the metal mounting, the door and the portal.

Returning to National Avenue we see the towering structure of house no. 115/24 on the corner of Spálená Street, which dominates the entire block behind it. The pleasant façade of this building attracts our attention, thanks to the presence of corner oriels and the tower with its coloured mosaic. The next two houses, no. 116/20 and no. 117, come from the workshop of František Buldra and date from some time after 1900. The obvious allegiance to the Art Nouveau creed of both buildings is manifested by the pheasant, the masks of young girls and the general disposition of the mass structure.

Národní třída (National Avenue) is the wide boulevard in the town centre connecting the lower part of Wenceslas Square and Na Příkopě with the river embankment. Most visitors to Prague will sooner or later take a stroll along National Avenue to see the National Theatre and, possibly, to do some shopping. This also provides an excellent opportunity to observe the beautiful Art Nouveau houses on the Old Town side of the avenue. They are the buildings of the former Topič Publishing House at no. 1010/2, and building no. 1011/7, which once housed a now defunct insurance company. The author of the highly decorative design of both houses was Osvald Polívka. The decoration of the houses is concentrated on the façades of the buildings and complies with the desire for urbane elegance and maximum visual effect. A similar concept has been seen already on Polívka's creation, U Nováků, on Vodičkova Street. Building no. 1011/7 has a conspicuous cornice with lateral gables of an unusual shape at both corners of the building. The cornice is supported by wall brackets and between them are five oblong window openings on which five Art Nouveau script letters spelling out "PRAHA" are drawn. All this is framed by a beautiful coloured mosaic with floral motifs. The central part of the façade is dominated by a glazed oriel with beautiful stucco decorations and at the sides are adorned with sculptures of owls. Another two narrow oriels with two windows and balconies are located on the lateral axes of the building. All three oriels are interconnected by a balcony on the first floor. The original purpose of the building becomes obvious once the inscriptions in the band above the oriel window, namely the words "WE INSURE", "LIFE", "CAPITAL", "RENT" and "DOWRY", written in Art Nouveau script on the mosaic background, are read. The visual impression of the façade is further enhanced by coloured glass basrelief under the main balcony and sculptures by Ladislav Šaloun on the gables and the attic.

The next house, no. 1010/2, was built in 1906-1908 by Polívka for the Topič publishing company. The name "TOPIČ" dominates the façade on both the balcony and the wall itself. This beautiful house has lateral axes crowned by oblong gables making niches, where yet again the name Topič is written on the ceramic mosaic background. Above the central part of the façade is a huge unsupported cornice and just below the cornice, between the windows, are beautiful wreaths with ribbons. On the first floor is a wide oriel with large windows and in the central part, as if built on top of this structure, is another narrower oriel with a balcony above it. On the baroque windowsill of the smaller oriel a coloured figural mosaic in a circular frame is located. The generous ornamental decoration featuring floral and figural motifs is placed against the green background on the second and third floors. The visual division of the façade is accentuated by individual parapet cornices.

Both houses are very colourful; the colours of the plaster, mosaics, sculptures, stucco work, etc., are those of the usual subdued hues of the Art Nouveau palette, but the glitter and beauty is added through the application of rich gilding.

The impressions of National Avenue culminate in the National Theatre building. This outstanding structure, built in the style of the Italian Neo-Renaissance, represents the dignified temple of national culture dominating the entire river embankment. The exterior sculptural decoration of the building bears the unmistakable hallmarks of the era of its origin. Perhaps only the roman chariots standing on top of the building seem to be a little out of step with the times.

The story of these sculptures is interesting because its present day form happens to be the work of several artists. The original models were prepared by Bohuslav Schnirch in 1888, but the task of finishing the work was entrusted to František Rous, Emanuel Hallmann and Ladislav Šaloun. The chariots carry three female figures, the goddesses of Victory. The whole sculpture was put in place in as late as 1910-1911 and Schnirch's followers left some Art Nouveau features in the completed sculptures.

Our current stroll through Prague ends at the Neo-Baroque Art Nouveau Bridge of Legions extending from National Avenue.

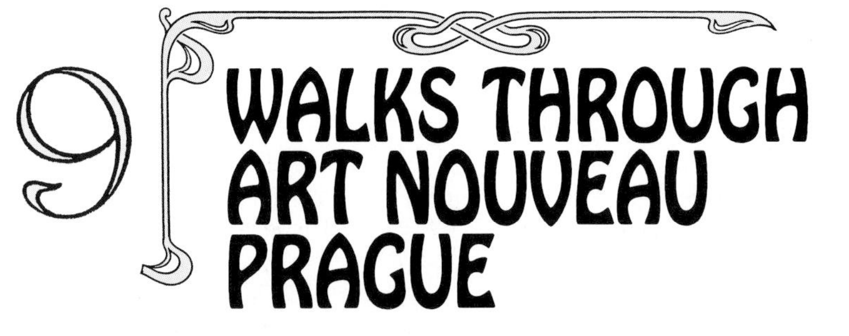

9 WALKS THROUGH ART NOUVEAU PRAGUE

A mascaron on one of the most "macabre" Art Nouveau structures in Prague, namely the Gothic Art Nouveau building at no. 234/26 Masarykovo nábřeží

One of the most beautiful, and possibly the most serene, walks through the inner part of the city is stroll along the right bank of the Vltava river. The scene of the attractive islands in the river, with Prague Castle and St. Vitus' Cathedral, is unparalleled in Europe. To draw our specific attention to Art Nouveau architecture we may start at the National Theatre, which can be reached comfortably on foot from Wenceslas Square in several minutes. Beside the National Theatre the river is spanned by the Bridge of Legions, built at the turn of the century on a design by Antonín Balšánek. The bridge is a fine example of the budding Art Nouveau influence in the style of Baroque-like objects. If we walk about halfway across the bridge and turn around, we see to our left the Old Town part of the embankment with the houses and palaces built in different historical styles. The late Neoclassical, Neo-Gothic and Neo-Renaissance styles can all be seen at a glance. Among the buildings occupying this part of the embankment, the most striking is probably the dark red structure of the Café Bellevue building, built in the style of the late Dutch Neo-Renaissance at the close of the 19th century. Further downstream we catch a glimpse of the Old Town Mills with Novotného lávka and the Smetana Museum, and the Charles Bridge with its Bridge Tower.

turn of the century. This part of the city used to be called St. Adalbert District, after the parish Church of St. Vojtěch (Adalbert) standing nearby. Further upstream from Jiráskovo Square to Palackého Square the former Zderaz district is located and yet further to the south lies the ancient district of Podskalí. All the above-mentioned names of districts are little more than names today. The original buildings and streets of these districts fell victim to a great redevelopment programme that included the rebuilding of the

Looking to the right we see two river islands, namely Střelecký Island, and somewhat closer to the bank, Slovanský Island. At the same time we may observe practically the entire New Town river bank, lined with houses from here as far as the Vyšehrad Rock. The section between the National Theatre and Jiráskův Bridge is full of proud, multistorey residences built in the Neo-Renaissance, Neo-Baroque, Neo-Gothic and Art Nouveau styles at the river embankment. Thus, several stages of the urban redevelopment programme obliterated the old Prague districts along the river for good. The old housing and roads were replaced by a new elevated embankment, and the new buildings have changed the nature of this part of the city to a considerable extent.

The beauty of the buildings makes the desire to inspect them from close quarters irresistible. Just behind the Na-

The frontispieces of buildings constructed in historicizing or Art Nouveau styles on the embankment between Jiráskovo Square and the Mánes building

tional Theatre in a little square, the two high Neo-Gothic houses no. 227/34 and no. 1648/36, built in 1906-1907 on a design by Gustav Papež, will certainly attract one's attention. The multitude of lancet and trefoil arches, oriels and gables above are a strange contrast to the calm dignity of the Neo-Baroque and Art Nouveau style of the house standing on the opposite side of the street bearing a distinctive green façade. Before going on, we shall look into a short street, Na Struze. There, on the corner (Na Struze and Vojtěšská Streets), stands house no. 230, built according to plans drawn up by Osvald Polívka. The style is Neo-Baroque and Art Nouveau in style, and the centre of gravity of the composition is the corner itself, with the oriel and towering superstructure above. The stuccos of two clown-like figures make a rather picturesque impression with their make-believe growth through the brackets supporting the corner oriel. Under the balcony on the wall look-

The sculptural decoration on house no. 224/32 is the work of the sculptor Ladislav Šaloun

Even the inscription on the portal at no. 235/28, “Vystavěno léta Páně 1904-1905” (“Built in the Years of Our Lord 1904 and 1905”), is part of the Art Nouveau frontal decoration

This stucco ornamentation on the Gothic Art Nouveau building at no. 234/26 would be impossible to reproduce. Two owls, typical Art Nouveau bird decorations, sit on the stucco tree decoration around the portal

ing onto Vojtěšská Street is a beautiful stucco of a winged sea horse. Above the balcony facing onto Na Struze Street one can find a stylized mask interconnected with drooping ribbons. This motif, in combination with the windowsill shaped into the two divergent volutes, evokes the feeling of a strange downward moion. The authors of the stucco work are most likely the sculptors Popp, Mayer and Riedl.

The corner of Na Struze Street and Masarykovo nábřeží is dominated by the huge corner house no. 224/32. The entrance gate and wide oriel with three partial window openings at floor level can be seen in the central axis of this street corner. The top of the oriel is formed by a spacious balcony with a wrought-iron balustrade. On the floor above is another smaller balcony supported by brackets. Thus, the visual impression of a very high building

The monumental staircase with ornamental pillars at house no. 235/28, and an example of Art Nouveau decoration on the banister

Both the magnificent decorative mosaic on the gable of the Hlahol Patriotic Choral Society building at no. 248/16, and its overall layout, are pure instances of Art Nouveau

is achieved. Above the main cornice the huge arched gable crowns the structure. It is decorated by Ladislav Šaloun's sculptures, and on top of the gable sits a gilded globe. The height of the building is further emphasized by the bronze sculpture of a mythical eagle set above the gable between two slender chimneys. The entire concept of the geometry of the façade ornamentation successfully aims to give the impression of great height, and thus the building dominates the whole block of houses standing immediately behind it. The tops of the two lateral faces of the building are adorned by large mascarons with massive floral and ribbon stucco decoration. The slightly elevated ground floor is decorated with band-shaped bossage of rather unusual decorative motifs which can be seen to repeat themselves also above all windows of the building. The entrance to the house makes a stately impression with its two lateral columns and the Goethe-Institut inscription above. The door frame is also massive and decorated with wrought-iron floral motifs identical to those found on the door itself. The attic above the sides of the building is enriched by a pair of decorative gables on both sides of this monumental structure. The lateral gables are decorated by stuccos of bunched flowers. The whole decoration creates the impression of there being yet another floor above the main cornice. The side facing the river embankment is enriched by a wide balcony resting on massive wall brackets. The whole decoration is supplemented by the customary Art Nouveau mascarons and wreaths. This Neo-Baroque Art Nouveau building, originally the head office of a now defunct Czech bank, was designed by Jiří Stibral in 1905.

The building next door, house no. 236/30, built in 1905, bears the inscription "The Guest's Home and God's Home". The architect obviously started by employing a Neo-Renaissance concept, as can be clearly seen in the façade paintings, the arched shape of the gable, and the disposition and the size of the windows. However, the stucco technique applied in depicting the floral decoration already shows the hallmarks of early Art Nouveau influences. Architectural sculptures displayed here depict lions as if walking out of the façade, and a sculpture of a knight stands in the niche of the central gable. The wall paintings are also interesting since they illustrate scenes from the river embankment reconstruction.

Another house, no. 235/28, was built in 1904-1905 by Matěj Blecha. The structure is essentially Neo-Baroque, and is supplemented by the Art Nouveau stuccos by Celda Klouček. In comparison with the previous buildings the façade of this house, with just one flat gable above the main cornice, seems to be rather plain. The façade decoration limits itself to horizontal bossing and some decorative elements at the entrance. The visual division of the façade dealt with by the presence of two small balconies with wrought-iron grilles. The height of the building is accentuated by strips of smooth plaster which run from both ends of the gable as far as the eaves. The entrance to the house, as well as the sides of the gable, are decorated by sculptures of infant figures standing under a stylized tree. In contrast, the interior of the house is quite imposing; the elliptical staircase is decorated with marble and the flights are supported by pillars with ornamental decoration on their capitals. There is also a beautiful floor mosaic in the corridor, with floral motifs in the centre and at the corners of the decorative pattern.

The next house, no. 234/26, is the example of a Gothic Art Nouveau building. The structure has three axes, and the larger gables rise above the lateral ones, which are optically emphasized by oriels spanning the first, second, third and fourth floors. The decorative effect of the façade is created by the presence of rich white stucco decoration (set in bands above and between the windows and in the balcony grilles) on the ochre background of the plaster itself. On the lateral tripled gables birds of prey are seated, whilst the topmost parts of the gables display Gothic Art Nouveau flowers. The entrance to the house is adorned by decorative trees, with owls sitting on their branches, that reach as high as the oriel above. Directly above the entrance the grotesque face of a mascaron preserves the peace of the house. Sculptured birds are present also inside the building. The beautiful stucco ceiling decoration has been preserved, as has the exquisite glass decoration of the door on the ground floor and mezzanine. The decorative grille of the staircase, and that of the door, are also very beautiful and original. This house was built in 1904-1905 on a design by Kamil Hilbert.

The corner building no. 233/1 is entered from Šítkova Street and is known as U Vávrů. The façade facing the river is decorated by two lateral oriels. Above the main overhanging cornice the sides and corners are decorated by high gables with lanced windows and decorative masks and floral ornaments. At the end of Šítkova Street is another corner building facing onto Vojtěšská Street. The building was erected in 1906 and bears the number no. 216/13. It is a school building built according to the plans of František Velich. The decoration of the façade corresponds to the building's purpose: the sculpture of St. Adalbert, the folklore and national motifs such as the Czech lion, a girl in Czech national costume, etc. The entrance portico features imitation bossing, over which there is either a coloured mosaic or a window with an etched floral motif.

A large part of Vojtěšská Street is occupied by the creations of Osvald Polívka. House no. 231 belongs to the Art Nouveau period of Polívka's professional life. Together with the neighbouring buildings, also the results of Polívka's Baroque-style work, it creates a uniform line of houses on the street, because its square Art Nouveau façade is broken up by a bossage and crowned with a Baroque-style gable. Here the stuccos of five human figures of varying statures are composed comparatively freely between the flights of the façade. Some of the figures are depicted as if they were comfortably leaning against the window frames. These basreliefs were probably created by Antonín Popp on the basis of drawings by Osvald Polívka himself.

Having viewed the immediate vicinity of the Church of St. Adalbert, which contains a number of interesting buildings, we return to the river bank, past three beautiful Neo-Renaissance buildings, Nos. 239/22, 238/20 and 237/18, built in 1905, and stop in front of the important building no. 248/16 named Hlahol, a typical example of Art Nouveau architecture. The house was built in 1905 on a design by Josef Fanta for the Hlahol Choir Association (the choir specializing in music with patriotic overtones). The dominating element of the façade is the huge arched gable with a coloured mosaic depicting an allegory of music and singing. The pair of human figures between the two bal-

Typical Art Nouveau frontal ornamentation - a mascaron, extensive vegetal embellishment and the figure of a woman - often found in close proximity under a bay window or balcony

conies on the first and second floors holds huge stucco wreaths. In the centre of the slightly elevated ground floor the Art Nouveau inscription "Hlahol" is set against a red background. Under the windows there are three bronze plaques with the names of important choir masters of the association - Karel Bendl, Karel Knittel and Bedřich Smetana. The right-hand portal is surrounded by a beautifully coloured mosaic depicting a bird with its wings extended. The rear of the building as seen from Vojtěšská Street is equally interesting. On the front gable stands the sculpture of a harpist. The façade is covered with inscriptions bearing a message on the aesthetic and moral values of singing for the nation and mankind: "The most precioust gift of singing is giving", "Where there is youth and heart, there is singing also", or "With a song for one's heart, and one's heart for one's country".

On returning to the river embankment we pass beautifully decorated buildings built in styles reminiscent of past times,

The preserved work of craftsmen and artists from the Art Nouveau period: the doors at the entrance to the Hlahol Patriotic Choral Society building

A fascinating evening view from Petřín Hill of the illuminated National Theatre and the Neo-Gothic and Art Nouveau buildings on Masarykovo nábřeží until we stop near the corner building opposite Mánes and the Šítkovská water tower. This beautiful large building, erected in Art Nouveau style by František Cuc in 1908, bears the number 2018/10. It has a wide, segmented arched gable, and above the main cornice an attic floor crowns the structure. The semicircular corner is composed of triple oriels with balconies and loggias in between. The façade facing the river is visually divided by a number of balconies with wrought-iron balustrades adorned by circular marks in bright colours. The colourful impression of the façade is enhanced by the tiles above the second-floor windows. Above the entrance gate the foliated tree branches extending from the face of a mascaron reach as far as a pair of figures of young women standing on either side of the portal.

Further towards Jiráskovo Square we pass several more buildings imitating historic styles. Leaving ehind the Jirásek Memorial we approach house no. 2000/78, (Two Thousand, Rašínovo nábřeží), named U Dvou tisíc which is interesting both in itself and because of the fact that it was built in 1904 by Václav Havel, the grandfather of current President of the Czech Republic. Some researchers believe that the design of this house, as well as that of its identical copy standing two doors only further up, was drafted by Osvald Polívka.

To walk from here to Palackého Square takes only about one minute. The Palacký Memorial, commemorating the Czech national revivalist and outstanding historian and politician František Palacký, dominates the area. In building the memorial the city of Prague wished to honour an important personality of our national history. During the selection of the best design for the memorial, the jury was most impressed by that submitted by the sculptor Stanislav Sucharda and the architect Alois Dryák. Sucharda's concept was to make the memorial tell the story of Palacký's contribution to national revival. The figure of Palacký himself in the middle is surrounded by many allegorical figures representing both past national defeats and triumphs of the nation's journey leading from the oblivion of national subjugation to national revival and final victory. The allegory is embodied in the helical structure of the individual sculptured figures crowned at the top by a figure representing Victory. The sculptural work was tested and perfected in 1905-1906 on half-sized models. The final work on the memorial was technically very demanding, since the rear group of figures was nine metres high. When working on the figures located in the monument's foreground, Stanislav Sucharda was assisted by the sculptor Josef Mařatka. The figure of Palacký himself was sculpted last. Originally Sucharda intended to use bronze, but he changed his mind and thus the principal figure of the memorial is made of stone; in the most experts'view this added further to the grand nature of the monument. The head of Palacký was sculpted by Sucharda himself from start to finish. The memorial was publicly unveiled in 1912, and represents the artistic expression of the heroic national fate.

From the park (Zítkovy sady) below the monument we can see the Emaus monastery and church, both of which date back to the reign of Emperor Charles IV. The complex of buildings (1924—1929) standing between the Emaus church and the park is one of the best examples of modern urbanism. The buildings were designed by architect Bohumil Hypšman. Another building worth mentioning is house no. 382, standing at the corner of the park and Dřevná Street. The building was erected in 1912 on the basis of plans drawn up by František Roith. Equally, house no. 390/42 should not be passed unnoticed since it documents the ability of the "modern" style to create a monumental building. The design was made by the formost representative of the Czech "modern" style, Jan Kotěra, and was accomplished in 1912-1913. The interior was designed by Kotěra's friend, Josef Zasche. The monumental appearance of the building is created by the stepwise division of the façade from the ground floor up to the pair of bands delineating the storeys of the building, and by the use of colours, which become gradually darker from the base upwards.

From here we head along the river as far as Vyšehrad Castle. This part of the river embankment was built at the turn of the century but was not fully completed until as late as the early twenties. This area used to be the district called Podskalí, the place where the wooden rafts travelling from the Bohemian forests down the Vltava river used to land, bringing wood to the city. The only surviving house from that period is the municipal customs building at Výtoň. The structure dates back to the 16th century and now houses a museum. Directly opposite the customs building is the Art Nouveau pavilion with a clock and a measuring device to gauge the water level in the river.

There is a tram stop at the old customs house at Výtoň, from where one can return to the National Theatre in about ten minutes. Those who are not yet tired can continue under the railway bridge (built in 1901) further upstream as far as the tunnel under the Vyšehrad Rock, built in 1902-1905 to connect the new suburban neighbourhoods with Prague. The project was prepared by František Velich, the then chairman of the Municipal Civil Engineering Authority. The style adopted is Romanesque cum Art Nouveau. Immediately behind the tunnel stands the maternity home built in 1911-1913 in Neo-Baroque style by architect Rudolf Kříženecký. Another point of interest is the group of several buildings built in Cubist style, standing between the railway bridge and the Vyšehrad Tunnel. This completes our inspection of the architectural treasures located on this side of the Vltava.

10 WALKS THROUGH ART NOUVEAU PRAGUE

Characteristic ornamentation in Art Nouveau blocks of flats featured carved doors with decoration above them. This example can be seen at house no. 1113/2 Dienzenhoferovy sady (Dienzenhofer Park)

Smíchov is one of Prague's oldest neighbourhoods, and bears the name of the village that once stood here. Smíchov can be reached from the city centre by crossing the Bridge of Legions spanning the river beside the National Theatre and turning to the left on the opposite side of the river. However, for the purpose of our current trip we shall take another route, leading from the National Theatre along the riverbank to Jiráskův Bridge, which connects the New Town with Smíchov on the opposite side of the river. The view from the bridge is breathtakingly beautiful. To the right we see the panorama of Prague Castle, the other bridges spanning the river and the green river islands. Immediately to our right, just behind the Mánes building and the ancient Šítkovská water tower, we find Slovanský Island; Střelecký Island is in the middle of the river, and further to the left we can see Dětský Island.

We can also spot the Lesser Quarter water tower situated to the right of the point at which Jiráskův Bridge meets Smíchov embankment. The most interesting part of Smíchov is the embankment itself, which starts at the Bridge of Legions and runs along the river as far as Palacký Bridge.

It can be noticed at first glance that the buildings between Jiráskův Bridge and the Bridge of Legions are older then those standing to the left of Jiráskův Bridge. The older houses were built mostly during the last quarter of the 19th century and were constructed for the most part in Neo-Renaissance style. The first Neo-Renaissance houses appeared in Smíchov during early 1860s, however, the greatest building boom came to Smíchov in the 1880s and 1890s. During this period not only pure Neo-Renaissance buildings were erected, but also buildings in the Neo-Gothic, and, later, in the Neo-Baroque style, were built.

As in other parts of the city, the intensity of construction activities was dependent on the prosperity of the urban region. The industrial expansion of Smíchov was the driving force behind the successful building proramme carried out at the beginning of this century. Smíchov was awarded municipal status in 1903 and was completely brought under the jurisdiction of the city of Prague in as late as 1922. At the turn of the century work on the construction of the stone embankment of the river continued on the Smíchov side with the same intensity as on the opposite bank. At the same time new streets and apartment blocks were founded, and due to the period of their origin these new structures were built mostly in Art Nouveau style. The part of Smíchov that is of interest to us can be delineated approximately by the following squares and streets: Dienzenhoferovy sady, V Botanice, Preslova, náměstí 14. října, Zborovská, Pecháčkova, Lesnická, Lidická a Janáčkovo nábřeží.

The Smíchov Market Hall on náměstí 14. října (14 October Square), dating from 1907-1908 and once a stunning Art Nouveau building, is still used as a market today

The Smíchov municipality (there were about 50,000 inhabitants in Smíchov at the close of the 19th century) had to resolve many problems stemming from the lack of social and commercial centres in the area. Therefore, a decision was taken to construct a National House and a Central Market Hall in the grounds of the former botanical garden. In 1905 the municipal council asked Dr. Alois Čenský to prepare a preliminary study of both structures, and having ap-

A view across the river to the magnificent apartment blocks on Janáčkovo nábřeží, whose façades shine with fresh plasterwork

proved the project the Council entrusted the execution of his plans to Dr. Alois Čenský. In view of the situation in the immediate vicinity of the two planned buildings, and bearing in mind their different purposes, it was decided that the frontispice of the National House should face onto Zborovská Street and that the Central Market Hall should look onto Preslova Street. Between the two buildings a public park was founded, connecting both structures into a single whole.

The National House was built in Art Nouveau style between 1906 and 1908 under the close supervision of Smíchov municipal council. Even today the building remains a magnificent focal point of this part of Smíchov. The huge central rizalit of the building faces onto Zborovská Street. Above the crown cornice rises the large elliptical gable with the sculptured allegory of Music at the top. The sculpture is by Josef Pekárek. This central part of the building boasts spacious windows to allow more the daylight to enter the main hall of the building. The roof of the building is partially hidden behind the gable, but its uppermost part rises higher than the gable and culminates in a tower-like structure. Pillars stand between the windows, their capitals richly decorated by Art Nouveau ornaments. Above the elevated ground floor is the balcony of the main hall resting on wall brackets. The ground floor is bossed and is optically separated from the rest of façade by a cornice. The building is entered from 14. října Square and from here the building looks most attractive. The impressive rizalit guards the entrace to the building on the ground floor. The entrance is protected by a typical glazed Art Nouveau marquee with spiral decorative motifs. The façade of the building is only modestly decorated with a floral ornament, and the dominant decorative feature remains the allegorical sculpture.

A detail of the interior décor of the National House in Smíchov: this head of a beautiful girl by Josef Mára is situated on the steps at the entrance

The interior of the building comprises a café and restaurant, rooms serving social purposes, and also club rooms. All the rooms were furnished in Art Nouveau style, making ample use of glass, marble, bronze and brass. The decoration of the interior was very even-handed and pure in its style. It is no wonder that two of the National House salons were awarded gold medals at the Prague Exhibition of Commerce and Crafts in 1908, as they quite obviously represented contemporary lifestyle and artistic taste extremely well. The task of decorating the interiors of the National House was placed in the hands of many renowned painters, sculptors and artisans of the time. For example, the paintings of figural motifs were executed by Láďa Novák, who, among other things, painted the decorations of the interior of the Hotel Evropa on Wenceslas Square. The busts resting on the pillars at the entrance staircase were sculptured by Josef

The mosaic designs in windows above doorways are the features which make Art Nouveau buildings in Smíchov, like this one on Zborovská Street, stand out

An Art Nouveau residential villa at no. 1078/30 Na Václavce Street from 1903, whose façade is decorated with paintings and stucco ornamentation

Mára. The brass lights were made by Franta Anýž on the basis of drawings by Alois Čenský. The wrought-iron balustrades, created on a design by the project director, were made by Malý & Company, and have been preserved to the present day. The decoration of several salons was supplemented by polished wood casing and by allegorical portraits of young ladies by Karel Špillar and Jakub Obrovský.

Unfortunately, the original decorations were mostly replaced by decorations owing their allegiance to the artistic clichés of the 1950s. However, a project to restore this historic monument to its original state is already under way. The Central Market Hall was built in the vicinity of the National House in 1907-1908. The building has a rectangular ground plan and is architecturally composed as a three-nave basilica. The central and highest nave (16.5 metres) is covered by a roof truss resting on twelve vertical pillars. The roof cover is made of slate. Daylight is allowed into the interior through the windows positioned in both faces of the nave and in the gables; there are also skylights in the roof. The vertical window panes are made of linear pressed glass, the skylight panes are made of wired glass and the frieze windows, entrance door and walls were glazed by pressed coloured glass. Both gable walls and the side belts of the nave were richly decorated with stucco work. The decoration of the building was destroyed during the 1950s for reasons similar to those applied in the case of the National House next door. During the 1970s the Market Hall was reconstructed into a retail outlet of standard supermarket type. Despite all these changes the building has retained its distinctly Art Nouveau character, and belongs to the group of unique architectural monuments in Prague. If the task of renovating the houses standing on 14. října Square is ever undertaken there will be an opportunity to create a unique architectural cluster demonstrating the influence of Art Nouveau architecture and decoration on civil engineering practices at the beginning of this century.

After completing our visit to the National House we may start a short inspection of the buildings standing in the vicinity of 14. října Square. We begin at the park at the end of Jiráskův Bridge. The most prominent feature of house no. 1102/1 is the façade with oriels facing the park. The entrance portal under the oriels is adorned with rich ornamental stucco decoration. The masks and the wrought-iron grilles on the balconies contribute to the unmistakable Art Nouveau flair of the building, despite the fact that technically speaking the house was founded on ordinary utilitarian principles. The same can be said of the majority of the buildings facing the park. The interior of the building is lined with well-preserved stucco decoration featuring yet another popular Art Nouveau bird, the swan. The decoration is supplemented with etched glass window panes on the staircase and a wrought-iron staircase grille. The rather unpreposessing house at no. 1113/2 is impressive in terms of the richness of its preserved interior decoration. Apart from the usual Art Nouveau stucco decoration in the entrance hall and in the corridors, we come across beautiful original carved apartment doors with fanlights above. The Art Nouveau furnishing of this house is complete and includes etched coloured glass, wreaths with ribbons, and a geometric grille in the staircase balustrade and even the plaques bearing the numbers of each floor are adorned with an engraved tree motif.

Next we inspect building no. 1117/6, erected on the opposite side of the park in 1905. The building has a high, original entrance door with windows in its upper part and with interesting original hinges. The frontal of the house is divided by two oriels on the second and third floors; under the main cornice is a rich floral ornament, and in the corners of the balcony balustrades stand sculptures of owls. The interior contains well-preserved original decoration.

Just across the street, opposite the National House, the corner of Zborovská Street and Lesnická Street is occupied by two houses with towering roofs. House no. 1156/8, built in 1908, has a protruding oblong oriel supported by a symbolic female figure. A sculpture of the Madonna and Child stands on the façade of the house. The entrance to the building is also interesting since it is abundantly decorated with stucco ornaments, reminiscent of the similar entrance to the Art Nouveau house at Jungmannovo náměstí in another area of the town. The circular window opening above the door is filled with a coloured mosaic of stylized flowers. Another house, no. 1154/6, is interesting because its portal is locked by a huge wedge-shaped anchor stone. From the lock grow flowers with ribbons and two infant figures lean against the arch of the portal. Similar decoration is repeated above the windows on the fourth floor. House no. 9 in Lesnická Street is distinguished by the triple-axial composition of its frontal. Balconies are located on the lateral axes. The Art Nouveau decoration is formed by vertical ornamental stucco bands on the façade. The balustrades of the balconies are also wrought into elaborate ornaments. House no. 1215/7, from 1910, differs from the others in that the decoration is accomplished by the application of smooth and coarse plaster in order to create interesting geometric ornaments. The balconies above the oriels in the lateral axes are guarded by mythical birds. The memorial on the wall informs us that Albert Einstein lived here in 1911-1912. The other houses in Lesnická Street (nos. 1214/5 and 1225/3) also have their façades enlivened by geometric ornaments and by wrought-iron balcony balustrades.

The corner buildings no. 84/9 (Lesnická Street-embankment) and no. 86/7 (Pecháčkova Street-embankment) might look familiar to many of us; both houses stand out from the other side of the river and are quite conspicuous owing to their neat and colourful façades.

The first of the buildings is a typical corner structure with a corner façade cupola and oriels on the lateral axes of both sides. The wooden casing of the oriel, as well as the horizontal and vertical wooden beams on the gable, are interesting and unusual features. The symbolic bird of this house is the owl. Inside the house the decoration has all the attributes of Art Nouveau décor: marble tiles along the staircase, mosaic windows and black, red, blue and white mosaic tiles on the floor. The house was built in 1909 by Emil Dufek. The second house is quite different, demonstrating how closely the Neo-Baroque and Art Nouveau styles stand side by side in the architecture of Prague. The façade is decorated with a wide range of ornaments, from simple geometric patterns to floral, animal and figural motifs. The ostentatiousness of the building is further emphasized by the rhombic corner oriel, crowned by a spire with battlements and tumbling decorative ribbons. The wrought-iron grilles on the balconies are twisted into spiral shapes, and masks support the main cornice. On the side facing Pecháčkova Street are female figures with floral decoration and between the flights bands of stucco basrelief employing a tree motif are situated. Through the entrance door with its mosaic window we enter the monumental hall with its marble staircase. The marble pillars on both sides of the staircase are decorated with tall wrought metal lanterns. The interior décor of the hall is supplemented by many utilitarian details made of metal, and by mirrors on the mezzanine platform of the staircase.

The whole block to the left is dominated by the huge building no. 855, dating from 1910. The plans was drawn up in 1909 by Richard Klenka and František Weyr. It is worth noting at this point that most of the construction activity in Prague was entrusted to renowned architects and that to learn from this heritage should be considered as a commendable habit even today. The house in question has a blunt corner façade topped by an attic with a large figural sculpture. The oblong balconies on the floor above the entrance portal are surrounded by polygonal oriels extending over the entire height of the façade. They form the structure which resembles the niche in the central axis of the building's façade. Behind the big segmented gable is a conspicuous system of chimneys similar to that on Stibral's house on the opposite river bank. The façade facing onto Pecháčkova Street tells a different story: here the oriel is located in the central axis of the building's façade. The façade is visually divided by cornices located at the elevations of individual flights and the coarse plaster is decorated with light-coloured areas filled with painted, Empire style patterns. The Empire style is also emphasied by the shape of the vases and their location at the corners under the attic.

Another building in Pecháčkova Street worth inspecting is house no. 1268/6. Here the most interesting element of the Art Nouveau decoration is the coloured mosaic in the window opening above the entrance door. The whole street is an example of an ordinary Art Nouveau apartment block with typical Art Nouveau façade decoration and with similar furnishings in the individual houses (nos. 1245/8, 1188, 1268/6). Despite all this, each façade has its individual flair. For example, the beautiful glass mosaics above the entrance to house no. 1242/4, together with their duplicates inside the building along the staircase, representing the pheasant - the most popular bird of the Art Nouveau style, cannot be surpassed.

Surprisingly enough, in this nest of Art Nouveau buildings near the National House many details of the original interior décor have survived to the present day. In most of these houses tiled staircases can be found, together with the original decorated window panes, etc.

That is the end of our short excursion around the environs of the National House in Smíchov. We may prolong our browse throught Art Nouveau Prague by visiting the remarkable Art Nouveau family villa situated in Na Václavce Street (no. 1078/30) not very far from here. The structure was designed by Alois Korda in 1903. On the façade of the tower we see a sundial. The tower itself is rectangular, with a circular lancet window opening and wooden balconies. The façade facing onto the street is decorated by paintings made directly on the surface of the plaster. The stylized floral pattern creates a very pleasant impression. The traditional stucco decoration is concentrated on the lateral face of the building. The villa bears the name Helenka.

Having come this far, it might be interesting to visit the Malvazinky cemetery. A number of tombstones there were carved according to designs by prominent artists such as Stanislav Sucharda, Jan Štursa, Čeněk Vosmík and Josef Václav Myslbek, to name but a few. The bronze sculpture Sacrifice, by Ladislav Šaloun, from 1920, stands in the cemetery grounds.

A colourful stained-glass window in one block of flats on Janáčkovo nábřeží in Smíchov

11 WALKS THROUGH ART NOUVEAU PRAGUE

Charming figural and floral stucco decoration on the façade of a typical Art Nouveau block of flats at no. 919 Janovského Street in Holešovice

This excursion will take us to the Holešovice-Bubny and Bubeneč districts of Prague, where, apart from having the opportunity to see many Art Nouveau structures, the visitor can spend some time at the Exhibition Ground or National Technical Museum, or simply admire an unusual panorama of the city from Letná Hill.

The area can be reached easily on Line C of the Prague underground network, and the journey will not take more the several minutes from the city centre. Alighting at Vltavská station, we begin our Art Nouveau journey at Strossmayer Square, dominated by the Neo-Gothic church of St. Anthony, built in 1908-1911. The plans were drawn up by the architect František Mikš. Opposite the church is the large building no. 990/4, the local school built in 1907. The sober Art Nouveau stucco decoration of the façade is in tune with the charming lateral gables bearing stucco views of the Czech countryside. Opposite the school stands the corner house no.978/9, built in 1907. The style of the building is a combination of the Neo-Gothic and Art Nouveau, and houses the restaurant U Zajíců. The Neo-Gothic portal bears the inscription Ave Maria, and is decorated on both sides by sculptures and Art Nouveau

floral ornaments. The same ornaments are repeated between the Neo-Gothic lancet arches above the windows.

Leaving Strossmayer Square and turning left, we find ourselves in Dukelských hrdinů Street, replete with Art Nouveau apartment buildings. House no. 969/6 is distinguishable by means of its Art Nouveau symbolic vases with flowers and sculptures placed both in the gable and between the windows. House no. 968/8 is decorated with floral ornaments and masks, while house no. 469/25 features a richly decorated portal with vases, stucco tree branches and wreaths. No. 470/27 bears a stucco mascaron above the entrance and the motif of a squirrel feeding on pine cones. House no. 471/29 bears the old-fashioned inscription "The First Civic Saving Bank In Holešovice-Bubny", and we find Art Nouveau decoration under the gable and on the façade. Another building, no. 967/10, built by Richard Klenka in 1909-1910, features a mascaron on the brackets above the oriels. No. 976/12 has interesting balustrades with wrought metal grilles, and no.

The Palace of Industry at the Prague Exhibition Ground was constructed in 1891 on a design by the architect Bedřich Münzberger for the National Jubilee Exhibition

Antonín Hrubý adapted this pavilion in the Exhibition Ground in Neo-Baroque and Art Nouveau style for use as the Lapidarium of the National Museum

975/14 is adorned by typical Art Nouveau masks and wreaths, and at the sides of the front gable by symbolic vases with stylized tree branches.

All these houses bear essentially the same kind of architectural decoration of the Art Nouveau period. Nevertheless, each of the buildings has its own individual character documenting the imagination of the ordinary contractors and decorators treading in the footsteps of the leading artists and architects of the time.

Houses constructed in other styles also stand on the Dukelských hrdinů Street. Just opposite the Park Hotel is a group of very beautiful buildings built in Neo-Renaissance style, with typically ornate wall paintings depicting scenes from Czech history.

Turning to the right we enter Šimáčkova Street, where the interesting houses in late historicism styles incorporating elements of Art Nouveau decoration can be found. The buildings worth noting are no. 915/18, no. 914/20, and especially no. 911/24, called U Kapličky, which bears likenesses of popular personalities from the Czech history.

Šimáčkova Street is intersected by Janovského Street, where we come across house no. 919/36. The building boasts conspicuous floral band-like stucco decoration on the façade. There are also wreaths with ribbons and small figural basreliefs in the middle of the large floral ornament on the house. The decoration stands out owing to the contrast of green plaster with red decoration.

Walking down Dukelských hrdinů Street we approach the Exhibition Ground. This vast area, founded in 1891, covers some 300,000 square metres. The reason for establishing the Exhibition Ground in Prague was the preparation for the Kingdom of Bohemia Royal Jubilee Exhibition, held in 1891. The occasion was seen as an excellent opportunity to give vent to the nationalistic moods of the time and to display the economic and cultural progress achieved in the Czech lands of the Empire.

The Industrial Palace was built to serve the purpose of the Exhibition. It is a large structure, 208 metres long with a total area of 12,870 square metres. Rather than using solid masonry, it was decided that a steel skeleton should be employed, as proposed by the architect Bedřich Münzberger. The technical design of the central skeletal part of the building was carried out by Ing. František Prášil, Chief Engineer at the First Czech Bridge-Building Factory, Prague. The weight of the steel parts making up the building exceeds 500 tones. The Industrial Palace was conceived as a permanent central

An allegorical group with the Prague coat of arms by František Hergesel, above the entrance to the Lapidarium

structure comprising eight main steel arches resting on the massive masonry corner pillars decorated with fanciful ornaments. Above the central section a decorative spire with a clock rises to a height of 51 metres. To the sides of the central part of the building the left and right wings of the Exhibition Palace are attached. The sculptures of genii above the entrance and the portraits of Czech technicians and inventors situated at the top of both wings of the palace were created by the sculptors František Hergesel, Antonín Procházka and Ludvík Wurzel. The elaborate, electrically illuminated water fountain designed by Ing. František Křižík has become the showcase of the Exhibition Ground. The architectural concept of the Exhibition Palace heralded the fall of the monopoly of the Neo-Renaissance, and the advent of the Neo-Baroque and Art Nouveau styles.

To the right of the main entrance to the exhibition area stands the Pavilion of the City of Prague, originally built in 1891 for the purposes of the Jubilee Exhibition and reconstructed in 1907 in Art Nouveau style by architect Antonín Hrubý. The building is decorated by frieze basreliefs by Gustav Zoula and allegorical sculptural groups by František Hergesel.

Under the Industrial Palace, near the footpath leading into the park, we find the pavilion built by Jan Koula, containing a panoramic view of the Battle of Lipany by Luděk Marold. The painting was installed in the pavilion in 1898, and soon became famous for its masterful illusion of the space and plasticity of the scene. Marold's panorama remains the favourite attraction of the exhibition area for visitors today.

Leaving the Exhibition Ground through the main gate and passing under the bridge ahead, we turn to the right and walk up the hill through Gerstnerova Street. The streets to our left are paradise for the admirer of Art Nouveau architecture, since the whole area was built at the beginning of this century and thus in the streets named Ovenecká, U Studánky, Sochařská, Malířská, Umělecká, Kamenická, Čechova, Šmeralova and Nad Štolou, many interesting structures are to be found. The majority of the buildings in this area are either of late historicizing styles with rich Art Nouveau decorations, or pure Art Nouveau architectural structures.

Items of special interest may include the buildings in Čechova Street such as nos. 307/27 and 300/25 built in 1910. The latter has an Art Nouveau interior with a typical ornamental iron grille in the staircase balustrade, its entrance is decorated by masks, and the corridor has the well- preserved, original mosaic floor tiles and ornamental friezes. The charming house at no. 296/23 features the triple-axial composition with decorated oriels. The metal balustrades and ceramic tiles above the windows (no. 286/21) are very pretty indeed. Some very important architects of the Art Nouveau period left their mark in Čechova Street. Antonín Balšánek built house no. 239/9. The façade of this house is asymmetrically divided by a shallow rhombic oriel with a balcony. The stucco decorations are located on the oriel and under the cornice. In 1908 Ferdinand Šamonil built house no. 282/16. It has a symmetrical frontispiece with a triangular gable and a corrugated cornice at the top. The stucco decoration is concentrated in prominent groupings above the windows. The exquisite houses. no. 295/20 and 294/22 were built by Václav Řezníček in 1909. The façade of the former building bears a variety of functional and yet decorative details. The central axis of the façade is completely taken up by an oriel with a balcony at the top; on the first floor a balcony extends across the entire width of the building's frontal. The other balconies are located on the lateral axes of the building. Niches at the sides of the oriel are decorated by sculptured female figures, and decorative basreliefs of infant figures are located in the gables situated on the lateral axes of the building. Inside the building, beautiful original etched glass windows have been preserved. The second house (no. 294/22), by Řezníček, is visually divided in precisely the opposite manner: there are two conspicuously protruding oriels located in the lateral axes of the frontispiece of the building. The central part of the façade is decorated by rich stucco ornaments, and the entrance to the building features pillars on both sides. A niche on the third floor contains a sculpture of Our Lady.

In the next street, Šmeralova, stand houses no. 360/30 and no. 378/28. The sober composition and decoration of both houses corresponds with the period of their construction: they were built by Václav Vacek in 1911-1912. House no. 378/28 has a remarkably massive overhanging cornice, and building no. 360/30 is adorned with neat ceramic decorations. Another specimen of the most popular symbolic Art Nouveau bird, the pheasant, is situated above the entrance to house no. 359/17, built by František Novotný and Antonín Mašita in 1911. House no. 358/19, built by V. Klatovský in 1911, is decorated by yet another variant of coloured tiles. No. 331/21 is recognizable from the mosaic motif of beetles, and our attention is drawn to house no. 297/13 by its prominent lateral oriels with spires at the top, and by its ornamental stucco decoration.

Leaving Čechova Street and crossing Milady Horákové Street, we enter Nad Štolou Street, situated at the upper mouth of the tunnel under Letná Hill. Heading towards the National Technical Museum, we should not neglect to take a look at house no. 951/10, adorned with rich stucco decoration. The next house, no. 950/12, is decorated with a beautiful coloured mosaic by Antonín Zámek (1906), depicting the Madonna and Child.

Our present excursion ends either with a visit to the interesting exhibits of the National Technical Museum, or simply with a stroll which enables us to admire the city of Prague from the elevated observation points along Letná Hill above the Vltava river.

A detail of the frontispiece of the National House in Karlín, dating from 1910-1911, by Josef Sakař; the decoration is the work of Antonín Štrunc and Oldřich Rákosník

The Karlín area of Prague is said to be a dirty industrial district, and a tourist guide or travel agency would probably only show the visitor the new Karlinn Hotel. But in this walk exploring Prague's Art Nouveau we shall take a much closer look at this area of Prague. If you decide to do some shopping in the best-known department stores in Prague, Kotva (The Anchor) and Bílá Labuť (The White Swan), you can combine business with pleasure. From Na Poříčí Street the Art Nouveau area of Karlín is only two underground stations away, from Florenc station to Invalidovna station. Alternatively, one can travel go by tram from náměstí Republiky (Republic Square) to Invalidovna in Karlín.

The first stop on our Karlín walk will be in a large park in which the complex of the former disabled soldiers' home is situated. It is only one ninth of an intended project designed by the Vienna architect Josef Emanuel Fischer von Erlach and constructed between 1731 and 1737 by Kilián Ignác Dienzenhofer. In front of Invalidovna stands a memorial to Count Peter Strozzi, who established the foundation for disabled soldiers in 1664. This creation, by the sculptor Moritz Černil, dates from 1898. With its monumental Baroque cum Neoclassical conception, and especially with its stately frontispiece facing the courtyard, Invalidovna creates a grandiose impression. The entrance hall contains plaster models of the statues of Generals Gallas and Bianchi by Thomas Seidan. Invalidovna is one of the most important monuments, not only in Karlín but in the whole of Prague, and is definitely worth a visit.

The Invalidovna parks are adjoined by the more recent Karlín district, which came into being at the beginning of the 20th century.

Yet Karlín is the oldest suburb of Prague, as its origins date back to 1817. It was founded on the flat Špitálské pole (Hospital field), a place that since the 10th century had witnessed a number of historical events. The district was named Karlín in honour of Karolina Augusta, wife of Emperor Franz Josef I. In the 19th century the suburb expanded, along with newly emerging industrial plants. At the beginning of the 1870s the first transport depot running omnibuses came into being in the district. The depot was soon equipped with trams, thanks to the effort of František Křižík, who moved his electric lighting plant there in 1884. In 1903 the status of Karlín was upgraded to that of an independent town, and it was only in 1922 that it was incorporated into Greater Prague. Despite modernization in this century, the district of Karlín has retained, in both its layout and in construction, the character of a town which was taking shape during the 19th century and at the beginning of the 20th century, at first in Neoclassical and Neo-Renaissance, and later in Art Nouveau style.

Directly adjoining the gardens behind Invalidovna are the buildings of greatest interest to us on our walk. The central area of this part of Karlín is Lyčkovo Square. In 1904-1906 a new school for the town of Karlín was built here.

This ornate stucco decoration on the façade of the Karlín school attests to the fact that Art Nouveau ornamentation met the requirements of the purposes for which buildings were employed at that time

The Karlín school building on Lyčkovo Square was erected in 1905 as one the most modern purpose-built structures of its kind

It is the grandest building in this part of the town, creating a grandiose impression and demonstrating how the town flourished at the beginning of the 20th century. It also illustrates how much local officials cared about the education of a new urban generation. When the commercial councillor and regional deputy, Jindřich Rouz, was elected mayor in 1902, he strived to have a decision to build a new school building adopted. The council invited tenders for building plans and selected the three best designs. But the construction costs seemed to be too high and therefore the architect Josef Sakař, who had been awarded second prize, was asked to adapt his plan. On the basis of this adapted version a final design and a budget were drawn up. The building was constructed by the builder Matěj Blecha, under the supervision of the architect Josef Sakař and in collaboration with a building committee. Building work began to take shape roughly at the end of the academic year and by the next academic year it had been completed and fitted out. It is also interesting that on 15 April 1906 the Emperor Franz Josef himself visited the place to see one of the newest and most modern schools in the monarchy (the school already had central heating, for example).

The Karlín school building is not, conceptually, purely Art Nouveau in style, but the names of its creators show an inclination towards the Art Nouveau style of architecture. The style is discernible in the functional nature of the building, as well as in its technological equipment and in the decoration of its façade. Old photographs also show Art Nouveau decoration in the interior. The school complex was erected in a place that corresponded to the town's intentions to situate the building such that it formed the front of a newly founded square named after František Rieger and stood at the foot of Vítkov Hill.

The main school building is imposing. It is three-axial and a there is a gable with a clock standing out above a stately central rizalit. Beyond it, on the same axis, rises a slender spire which makes the building look even taller. An attic balustrade diverges in both directions from the front gable above the whole length of the main cornice. Below the main cornice, on the central rizalit is a sign "Built A. D. MCMV," and coloured town emblems. Within the whole school complex the separate central building creates the impression of a monumental central rizalit, as there are lower wings forming an obtuse angle with the back of the main building, which then turn through a right angle and open the whole complex out towards the square. Both wings have front and side façades topped with gables and an attic balustrade above the main cornice. Together with the central building, the bent wings form an enclosed space for the courtyard. This also had its significance, as the axis of the main building divided the school into the boys' and the girls' area. The sculptural ornamentation of the school was the work of sculptors Antonín Štrunc and Antonín Mára. The most notable is the sculptural decoration of the main gable of the main building, and paintings on the façades of the wings. On the gable above the central rizalit of the chief building is a sculpture of St. Wenceslas in rich Art Nouveau stucco vegetal decoration. Both main entrances to the building are decorated with more sculptures and with glazed mosaic panes. The central part of the main building bears a sculptural relief of Jan Amos Komenský (Comenius) with lavish vegetal stucco decoration. Art Nouveau stucco decoration also appears on the façade of the main building, as well as on the wings. The decoration is outstandingly beautiful and technically pure around the clock on the gable, around the entrances, above the window openings (made into a mare's head) and on the sides of the main building. As for the wings, they are especially noteworthy for their coloured paintings depicting scenes from Czech history. The painting of the left wing depicts the military leader Jan Žižka with Prague behind him, and the painting on the right wing illustrates the coronation of Ferdinand Dobrotivý as king of Bohemia. In Hybešova Street, in front of the Kaizlovy sady expanse, stands Národní dům (The National House). As well as in other towns, the National House became in its time an expression of municipal representation. Its construction was decided upon by the municipal council in 1907. It began on a small Invalidovna meadow in March 1910, and by 1 May 1911 a small restaurant had opened on the ground floor. The building was designed by the architect Josef Sakař, and was built by architect, Otakar Nekvasil. It is a three-floor house in Art Nouveau style standing in an open space, segmented by rizalits, and the width of the building varies according to its height. It is only sparsely decorated with sculptural ornamentation by Antonín Štrunc and Oldřich Rákosník. Relatively plain plastering is embellished by coloured oval-shaped tiles. The window openings above the terrace are also oval in shape. The surface of an arched gable is decorated with a figurative and geometrically segmented motif and figures of children are situated in the corners of the terrace railing above the main entrance. With some small exceptions, the craft and construction work, including the internal equipment, was effected by local craftsmen and tradesmen. The interior of the building contains a monumental staircase, whose landing opens onto the terrace in the front, below which is the main entrance. The staircase is tiled with Slivenet marble and was designed

The broad front gable of the National House in Karlín, located on Hybešova Street, features figural and geometrically shaped decoration

Pretty, colourful sculpted ornamentation beneath a bay window and the balcony decoration containing a mask at no. 435/109 Křižíkova Street

in such a manner that it could also be used by a theatre which was to have adjoined the building. A place next to the building was reserved for the theatre and was provisionally adapted as a park. The house had electric lighting, and was heated by steam and warm air. The Karlín National House was built as a stately public centre of the new part of Karlín and followed the example of other suburbian districts, especially Smíchov, Vinohrady and Nusle.

The surrounding apartment buildings were strongly influenced by Art Nouveau architects and builders. House no. 519/5 in Hybešova was built by Emil Králíček and Matěj Blecha in about 1910. Next to it, on the corner with the Na Střelnici, the next striking feature is Art Nouveau house no. 521/6, dating from 1910. It otherwise simple façade is horizontally ornamented with friezes and adorned with regularly repeated blue square tiles. All in all there are several houses containing similar decoration in this part of Karlín. There is a remarkable house no. 1, from 1912, on the corner of Hybešova and Kubova Streets. It boasts a façade with coloured glazed tiles combined into horizontal and vertical bands, and below the main cornice the tiles form whole patterns. The decoration of the corner frontal is supplemented by a painting with a folklore figure and a sign, "Pax Salus". In the interior the house contains coloured mosaic windows on the staircase and mosaic tiling. The neighbouring house, no. 527/3, differs only in the colour of its plastering and the ceramic decoration used. House no. 529/7 has richer and more segmented Art Nouveau decoration. The house has an angular bay window and above it is a balcony with grilles shaped into spirals with ribbons. Above the windows appears a mask, a typical Art Nouveau element. The centre of the decoration is again an oval-shaped ceramic tile. In nearby U Invalidovny Street we should especially notice house no. 525/7 (architect R. Pecha), and in Na Střelnici Street house no. 528/4 with a front bay window, and especially outstanding multilayered stucco, above all from the second storey upwards.

At house no. 526/4 in Kubova Street, adjoining a corner house, we can once again compare the ceramic and tile decoration of its façade with the ornamentation of the neighbouring houses. The house has an interesting oval window on the gable. Art Nouveau house no. 505/6 has been acknowledged as a listed building; it is the work of the builder František Šimůnek, dating from 1908, with paintings by Karel Klusáček based on sketches by Mikoláš Aleš. The paintings depict various birds painted against a red background, such as a swan and a stork. The segmentation of the façade is accentuated by a combination of smooth plastering and rough brickwork. The interior is known in particular for its fine mosaic tiling and glass mosaic of Karlštejn Castle above the entrance.

Lyčkovo Square is surrounded mainly by houses in Art Nouveau style. House no. 472/8 has an outstanding relief of the Madonna and Child and angels, and the entrance is again guarded by a mask. The stucco wreaths and branches with fruit above the windows accentuate the decorative style of Art Nouveau. Houses no. 411/9 and 462/10 are also worthy of note. They were built before 1906 by Václav Romováček and Bohumil Štěrba. There are loggias standing out beautifully on a bay window covered by a wooden roof. The shaped grilles are also remarkable. House no. 464/17, dating from 1906, and situated round the corner in Křižíkova Street, has a simply ornamented façade. Nevertheless, the contrast of its coloured plastering and dark red facing around the windows produces an interesting impression. The original door in the interior is carved. On Art Nouveau house no. 452/4 we may still read the gilded signs "Sculpture, stucco, studio of O. Rákosník". Below its bay window is a sign that reads: "In beauty there is consolation". The signs and decorations reveal the occupation of the owner. House no. 435/109 is in Gothic and Art Nouveau style. The whole range of Art Nouveau decorations is displayed in combination with sharp Gothic elements. A pointed Gothic balcony is supported by a figure with a huge stylized tree and fruit, and the omnipresent ribbons, heraldic plates with vegetal decoration below the windows, and owls sitting on branches. The onlooker will certainly like the beautiful and fine panelling of the top balcony.

Certain details of the houses merit closer examination. House no. 612/68, otherwise in a very bad state, has a remarkably shaped metal grating. The façades of houses no. 488/115, standing on the corner of Křižíkova and Březinova, and no. 463/113, built in 1905 by Alois Stárek, are also interesting. We should pause by house no. 489/66, a Gothic-style Art Nouveau building dating from 1905. A figure representing a Hussite captain stands out on the corner. The combination of historicizing Gothic and Art Nouveau is most striking in the spaces above the compound Gothic windows filled with vegetal stucco ornaments. As for animal sculptures, owls and frogs stand out very effectively on the gable. Houses built in around 1905 and displaying elements of Art Nouveau decoration can be also found in Urxova Street; for example, house no. 458/8 contains typically Art Nouveau decoration with branches and wreaths that stand out in relief. The corner of Urxova and Petra Slezáka Streets is formed by Art Nouveau house no. 483/5. It has a notable prism-shaped corner tower with a pair of bay windows containing excellent details of typical mascarons and metal consoles with vegetal motifs. The construction of the tower is also Art Nouveau in style, made up of a prism that goes through a disc and is topped with a helmet. Both fronts are segmented by vertically placed rectangular slabs. A figurative stucco element is placed between the windows of the first floor facing Urxova, under a segmentally arched roof. It represents a female figure in national costume carrying a child with a halo, most probably a folkloric Madonna and Child. This Karlín house is a legacy of the prominent architect Osvald Polívka, who built it in 1905. Charming Art Nouveau decorations can also be found in Petra Slezáka Street, for instance those of house no. 446/13 from 1911, or of nos. 531/14 and 445/15. On our way to Křižíkova underground station we will certainly note the 1909 Art Nouveau house no. 504/24 in Šaldova Street, which stands out as a result of the typically Art Nouveau elements of its decoration - branches and the shaped metal balcony grilles. The house containing private flats at no. 492/34 Šaldova Street was designed in 1902 by the architect Alois Čenský, a famous author of the Art Nouveau Vinohrady Theatre. Another interesting building is house no. 493/10, dating from 1907, boasting fine vegetal stucco decoration on its façade and a relief figure of St. Wenceslas, the patron saint of Bohemia, with a sign "Nedej zahynouti nám ni budoucím" (May neither we nor our future perish).

13 WALKS THROUGH ART NOUVEAU PRAGUE

A colour mosaic in the window above a door in the insurance building located on Vršovické Square, Vršovice, erected in 1911-1912 in Art Nouveau style

A tram ride takes us to another Prague castle, also historically important and shrouded in myth. We take the tram from the National Theatre and travel along the Vltava embankment to a railway bridge under Vyšehrad. The stop where we alight is called Na Výtoni. The slender towers of the Neo-Gothic Church of SS Peter and Paul are visible from a distance. A tour of the church will enable us to admire the well-known panel painting of Our Lady of the Rain (Panna Marie Dešťová), a relic already in existence before the reconstruction of the church. It is situated in the third chapel on the right and is a Bohemian work of art from the middle of the 14th century. The contents of the church are mostly Neo-Gothic, but we can find some Art Nouveau elements as well, the most interesting of which is the altar of the Bohemian patron saints in the second chapel on the left, the work of Jan Kastner. However, Art Nouveau is most showily manifested in the ornamental and figurative murals created by František and Marie Urbanovi in 1902-1903.

The most striking features of the stucco ornamentation on the façade of building no. 432/27 (Jaromírova Street) are the large masks of girls' faces on the eaves

The most visited place in Vyšehrad is its cementery, dominated by the pantheon (Slavín), a mass grave of Czech artists and politicians. The architectural arrangement of the pantheon and arcades around the cemetery was designed by Neo-Renaissance architect Antonín Wiehl, and the whole complex also creates a Neo-Renaissance impression. But in spite of this, the artists of an Art Nouveau epoch have left behind them a significant legacy in their funeral ornamentation.

The beginning of the 20th century constituted a significant turning point in the way in which the ornamentation of tombstones was dealt with by sculptors and stonemasons. The sepulchral sculpture underwent changes in conception: a number of prominent sculptors became interested in the motifs of life and death, and expressed their artistic and human beliefs more freely and decoratively. Their works of art, often very mature, through which they paid tribute to

The tombstone of composer Antonín Dvořák by Ladislav Šaloun in the so-called Wiehl Arcade at Vyšehrad Cemetery

the dead, can be found in the Vyšehrad cemetery in large numbers.

A representative of Czech symbolism, František Bílek, created for the grave of the writer Václav Beneš Třebízský a symbolic above life-size statue called "Sorrow", represented by a female figure. A bronze relief, "Christ the Pilgrim on the Way to the Cross", by the same sculptor, can be found on the grave of the Šebek family. The most effective funeral sculpture is Bílek's work entitled "Strávena tvým ohněm, utonula jsem v tobě" (Consumed by your fire I have drowned in you).

As for other representatives of Art Nouveau style in Czech sculpture, Ladislav Šaloun demonstrated his artistry in the ornamentation of the tomb of composer Antonín Dvořák. Following the principles of Art Nouveau, he covered the whole tomb with monumental decoration, and placed a bust of the composer in the centre. He also elaborated the background. Šaloun further participated in creating a tomb for the Jeřábek family. He is an author of a bronze relief of the Holy Trinity, dominated by Christ on a double cross. The whole ornamented monument, with the recurrent motif of a stylized lily, was designed by the architect Josef Fanta. The tombstone of Jan Topinka, dating from 1897, is one of Šaloun's funeral busts. His last work on the cemetery can be found at the grave of the Míla family, and comprises a white marble statue of a woman scattering roses on the grave.

The work of sculptor Bohumil Kafka is also present at Vyšehrad cemetery. Especially impressive is a sculpture from 1907, "Objetí lásky a smrti" (An Embrace of Love and Death) on the grave of Josef Kaizl. The artistic basis of the monument is in the synthesis of naturalistic modelling with a literary idea in a symbolic shape of the Angel of Death. In 1904 Kafka also created a statue of the Angel of Death for the Jirásek family. Kafka's sculpture, the Our Lady of the Shepherds on the tombstone of the Tichý family, dates from 1912. Kafka's bronze statue of a mourning angel is situated on the marble tomb of the Wohanka family; Celda Klouček collaborated on its monumental Art Nouveau decoration. Sculptural decoration by Stanislav Sucharda can be found on the tomb of the Milde family, and a bronze portrait locket also created by him is located on the memorial to the poet Adolf Heyduk. Sucharda's own grave is also situated at Vyšehrad. It was designed by Ladislav Machoň, and has a gravestone and its own sculpture.

In memory of the poet Svatopluk Čech, Jakub Obrovský created a half life-size statue in 1908. The memorial commemorates a well-known book by the poet called "Ve stínu lípy" (In the Shadow of the Linden Tree). The tomb of the Pacák family is particularly eye-catching; beside it kneels a weeping woman and a man in costume by František

The statue entitled "Sorrow", on the grave of the writer Václav Beneš Třebízský, by the master of Czech symbolism, František Bílek

The decoration on the Vršovice Insurance Building was created by Ladislav Šaloun, Antonín Štrunc, František Úprka and Jakub Obrovský

Úprka. A symbolist sculpture portraying a falcon that has been shot down is also represented on the grave of the Sokol movement official, Franta Kukla.

Surprisingly, the relatively short Art Nouveau era has left prominent traces at Vyšehrad cemetery, especially in its inclination towards decoration, symbolism and stylization. Amongst other Art Nouveau tombs is, for example, a tomb of the king and emperor's court councillor, Jiří Pacold. It dates from 1907 and displays a wreath of foliage and superb candle lamps. A motif of a mourning woman can be also found on the grave of the Hübner-Pelnář family. Other items of interest include Art Nouveau metal flowerpots on the grave of the Pupp and Štorch family, and the lamps on the graves of Bohumil Živna and the Šnobls. The graves of the Kettner and Nekvasil families, as well as the Chudoba, Srb and Lužický family tombs, were also designed in Art Nouveau style.

After a general tour of Vyšehrad and a rest in this quiet place surrounded by greenery we can observe the town from St. Leopold's Bastion. From here we can see the New Town with its churches from the period of Emperor Charles IV, and further to the right is the Nusle Valley with the Botič river running through it and with a dense network of apartment houses. It is in the Nusle valley, visible from our present vantage point, that our exploration of the Art Nouveau style of architecture will continue.

We leave Vyšehrad by the Tábor Gate (Táborská brána) and turn left under Vyšehrad along Lumírova Street. We leave behind the Baroque Vyšehrad wall on the left; the houses on the right date mostly from the end of the 19th and the beginning of the 20th century. Of special interest among them is no. 452/9, an Art Nouveau house called The Bohemian Crown (U České koruny). We now walk under a railway line to Ostrčilovo square, on the edge to the Nusle valley. The walls on the hill in front of us are the remains of the original 14th-century Gothic city fortifications. We should not fail to notice the corner hotel with a light green façade. The hotel, no. 462, was designed and constructed in 1906 by the builder Jaroslav Benedikt, who also built other Art Nouveau houses in the vicinity of the hotel below Vyšehrad. According to contemporary sources, the hotel has had the same name since it was erected. There is stucco decoration in the restaurant, on both entrances to the building and also in the rooms on the second floor which face onto Ostrčilovo Square. A sunflower has been used as the most common motif of the decoration. The rooms originally had tiled stoves, but this Art Nouveau work has not, unfortunately, been preserved. The hotel interior contained decorative window panes in the rooms, and etched window panes graced the corridors and staircase. The largest window pane, 120 by 300 centimetres in size, decorated the lounge. The hotel also contained a hunting hall. It was modernized in the 1940s and adapted to a design by the architect František Matějíček, who was also the architect, amongst others, of house no. 789 in Nusle. The Union Hotel was taken over by the firm owned by Josef Rejzek in 1910, and after November 1989 it was returned to the grandson and namesake of the former owner, Josef Rejzek. The devastated hotel underwent complex reconstruction work in 1992 and is now a top-quality hotel. The reconstruction work was carried out by Českomoravská stavební společnost s. r. o., on the basis of the construction plans of a design agency belonging to Josef Miňovský, the architectural design having been made by architect Jan Štípek and academic architect Antonín Jeníček. During reconstruction the stucco decoration in the café and the entrance was restored. Some of the preserved window panes dating from the beginning of the century were used to decorate the basement wine cellar, located on the site of the original cellars. The interior is decorated in Art Nouveau style; the restaurant and café are dominated by brass elements and chandeliers. The windows face the monumental brickwork walls of the Vyšehrad fortress, and the New Town city wall reminds us of the ancient history of Prague.

To the right of the Union Hotel, at the corner of Sekaninova and Oldřichova Streets, stands a large house dating from 1910 and boasting distinctive Art Nouveau façade ornamentation, with outstanding mascarons in the shape of satyrs. On the front gable a huge stucco relief illustrating a scene from Bohemian mythology stands out: a strong Bivoj carries a boar on his back.

There are several houses in Oldřichova Street with predominantly Art Nouveau decorations and a recurrent use of mascarons, mainly the satyr. We recommend that the visitor take a closer look at houses 427/31 and 489/4, and especially the huge mask on house no. 541/12, dating from 1911. House no. 383/26 displays typical Art Nouveau ornamentation, and we will also certainly notice house no. 512/42, with masks on the gable and mythical birds holding the ends of an Art Nouveau stucco semi-wreath.

On Nezamyslova Street, which runs perpendicular to Oldřichova, stands another Art Nouveau house, no. 407/8. Its façade demonstrates that even the well-planned date of construction - in this case the year 1906, inscribed on a relief stucco ribbon - had become an organic part of the decoration of houses in Art Nouveau style. There are floral ornaments in semi-arched ledges around the windows, under the windowsills they are repeated in bands, and the balcony panelling is also made of stucco. The central front gable rises above the attic of the house. Thinner lateral axes are topped with an inlaid main cornice which is supported by four sculptures of little owls, rather than by the usual consoles.

Let us now have a look at Jaromírova, a major artery which carries tram traffic. The façade of the house The Golden Rose (U Zlaté růže) at no. 557 contains all the motifs of Art Nouveau decoration - wreaths of foliage, spirals, oval-shaped tiles. The front of the house is ornamented by rich stucco decoration in bands and in the very centre is a stucco relief of married couples exploring local history on a walk in the Czech countryside. A few dozen metres further on we notice similar Art Nouveau houses adjoining one another. House no. 433/25 has an attractive sign, "Nám dobře, nikomu zle" (Let us be well and no-one unwell), and its front is dominated by a sculpture of an archangel and a motif of a tree with a snake in the garden of Eden. House no. 432/17, and the adjoining house no. 431/29, are identical, the panelling of the balcony railings is made up of wreaths, and again there are mythical birds on the façade above the main cornice. House no. 430/31 also differs from the others in that it features a cross made up of ornaments. A bird is sitting on the cross and huge masks of young girls look down from the façade. The element of a smiling mask is also repeated on a neighbouring house, no. 21/33, dating from 1908. In addition, the house has charming balconies with elaborate forged grating. Elements of Art Nouveau decoration can be also found on the opposite side of the street.

We now leave the picturesque Nusle valley, the streets of which bear the names of individual members of the Přemysl dynasty, and through Křesomyslova Street we enter the part of Nusle centred around Bratří Synků Square. The short, steep Sezimova Street leads out of the square and where it begins stands an interesting Art Nouveau house, no. 481/15. Its smooth façade, segmented only by its geometric ornamentation, is dominated by an outstanding Art Nouveau motif on the frontispiece: a relief of a female figure, her arms outspread and a flowing robe transformed into the shape of a peacock. The building was created in 1908 by Karel Hannauer Senior, who also designed post-Art Nouveau blocks of flats, for example no. 45/9 Boleslavova Street. This corner house from 1913 is a synthesis of former Neo-Baroque and Art Nouveau decorations with Cubist elements. The house still outshines the others through its modernism and the functionality of the exterior, and more especially the interior. Walking around the Neo-Renaissance building of the Nusle Town Hall, we find ourselves on Pařížské komuny Square. Houses no. 554/1 and 545/3, dating from 1911 and situated above the Town Hall, have relief stucco sculptures and masks on their façades. We continue along Svatoslavova Street to Vladimírova, where there are two houses of note, namely nos. 59/14 and 567/11 from 1911, forming a wide corner with Nuselská Street. Their façades are ornamented by fine vegetal motifs.

We now walk back to Bratří Synků Square and take a tram on Otakarova, which will take us two stops to Vršovice where we get off by the Bohemians Stadium. In a few minutes we can walk along Sportovní Street to Vršovické Square. Behind the Church of St. Nicholas (kostel sv. Mikuláše) is building no. 67, erected between 1911 and 1912 as an Art Nouveau style savings bank and an block of flats. It was designed by the architects Antonín Balšánek and Josef Bertl, and decorated by the sculptors Ladislav Šaloun, Antonín Štrunc, and František Úprka, and the painter, Jakub Obrovský. The front gable of the building is dominated by the emblem of the town of Vršovice and large figural sculptures, down from which flows a massive loose Art Nouveau wreath; this motif is repeated, with several variations, in the decoration of the whole building. The space in front of the main entrance with two high columns on which bronze sculptures of eagles are perched, was designed as a resting place with seats. The main hall of the savings bank is lined with marble, and we should note the Art Nouveau memorial tables on both sides. Above the en-

The ceramic sculptures of children bearing wreaths form part of the décor surrounding the stairs leading up to the administrative section of the insurance building in Vršovice

trance to the lounge there are recurrent wreaths, and the space is embellished by a coloured ceramic mosaic. The glass ceiling of the lounge is supported by columns with decorated capitals and between them, around the whole perimeter, are plaques and masks joined together by vegetal ornaments. Two life-size sculptures decorate the arched entrance. The remaining space, as well as official rooms inaccessible to the public, is decorated with Art Nouveau motifs. Among them are superbly inlaid mosaic windows and doors with etched motifs in the panes, corner protectors, doorplates, security grilles, and even the furniture, which has been partly preserved. The most stunning Art Nouveau decoration is the ornamentation of the staircase leading to the first floor, which begins with marble pillars with ceramic sculptures of children who are again holding loose wreaths, and a wooden staircase banister with carved Art Nouveau ornamentation. We should not forget to look at the side entrance to the building, above which is a glass mosaic window open-

The insurance building in Vršovice at no. 67 is the Art Nouveau creation of architects Antonín Balšánek and Josef Bertl

ing in typical Art Nouveau colours. The entrance hall also includes a pretty, impressive brass and glass chandelier. A coloured mosaic has also found a place above the door to the courtyard.

Above the Vršovice Savings Bank extends the upper part of Vršovice, an elongated wedge-shaped area between Moskevská and Ruská Streets, which narrows as it approaches Slovinská Street and includes, for example, Kodaňská, Norská and Krymská Streets. Upper Vršovice acquired its present shape after 1894, and until the formation of the Czechoslovak state construction activity flourished. Each block of houses was a separate unit completed on both sides by enclosing elements - a bay window, a bevelled corner with an attic and gable, and a tower.

In Moskevská Street we find a number of typical Art Nouveau blocks of flats, which have a somewhat uniform decoration on their façades: similar stucco wreaths between the windows, a house with one or two bay windows, and metal balcony railings containing geometrical patterns. House no. 267/51 has more distinctive, lavish decoration, with figurative reliefs on the first floor and above the second floor which allegorically depict various artistic and agricultural activities performed by men. We should rightly stop to take in two large, connected five-floor houses on the corner of Moskevská and Slovinská Streets (no. 262/57, 1-3), which dominate Svatopluka Čecha Square. They are especially valuable examples of late Art Nouveau architecture and the individualistic modern movement. They were erected between 1911 and 1913 by the building firm of Václav Čáp. The house is topped on both sides of the corner with a segmented gable and a thin arched awning. Its façade,especially above the main frontal, is strictly geometrically and functionally segmented, and squares with geometrical ornaments recur only between the windows on the storeys. The interiors of house should be noted for their refined artistic and craftsmanlike details. At the other end of Moskevská Street stands Art Nouveau house no. 77, dating from 1909-1910. It architecture reveals that it was designed by an experienced architect, in this particular case by Osvald Polívka, the author of several designs in Ruská and Kodaňská Streets. In Ruská Street, houses no. 470/6 and 473/8 were designed by Polívka. Both of them are examples of the architect's tendency to move away from "Baroque-style Art Nouveau" and to move towards geometrical Art Nouveau. The houses have a completely flat façade, segmented only by geometrically different sculptural structures. House no. 473/8 has interesting fan-shaped rustic motifs around the windows. Within the overall composition, besides the Art Nouveau "decentralization" arising out of

One often comes across beautiful examples of artistic work and crafsmanship - such as this ceramic picture - inside terraced blocks of flats

the emphasis upon the lateral axes of the frontispiece, "centralization" resulting from a certain accentuation of the central axis by means of the front gable, is also applied. In both houses sculptural ornamentation has been incorporated into the structure, and no. 473 also has a polygonal bay window, which in this context represents a contrasting historicizing element. The stucco work is, in both cases, an example of outstanding Art Nouveau architectonic relief. House no. 473 has a clearly defined space with two figures - a male with a violin and a female singing - very closely attached to the portal. The national costumes, along with the symbols of music and a sign "Kde domov můj" (Where my home is) embody our national anthem. The stucco work on house no. 470 also has patriotic undertones. It is basically an ethnographic genre treated in a high relief and placed on a rectangular niche. The façade includes other interesting fine stucco sculptures which create a very pleasant impression, for example consoles in the shape of frogs (this time a satisfied frog that has just had a good lunch - a charming element of Polívka's inspiration drawn from the world of fairy tales) or portrait heads in a decorative framework on the ground floor. Other interesting examples of lavish stucco decoration in Art Nouveau style can be found in Ruská, on houses in historicizing styles such as no. 567/28, a Neo-Gothic-style house with rich stucco sculptures, especially below the bay window.

There is another house designed by the architect Osvald Polívka at no. 444/11 Kodaňská Street. The house is in a relatively bad state at present, yet its façade still displays outstanding Art Nouveau decoration in the form of rich floral ornamentation, especially huge individual stylized flowers in the central section of the frontal, or animal symbols between the windows. Here one finds charming squirrels, and there are female heads in the circle above the windows, which have replaced the usual mascarons. Although its rich floral decoration is suggestive of trends at the turn of the century, the use of the contrast between smooth plastering and rough brickwork corresponds more to the subsequent period of the more austere and sober architectonic Art Nouveau.

The less informed observer might feel that Kodaňská Street creates a similar impression to the stately Pařížská Avenue in the Old Town. This "little Pařížská" is a display of Neo-Gothic and Neo-Renaissance houses, abounding in spires and turrets, with segmented and very different gables. We can even find here grand Neo-Baroque houses with rich architectonic sculptures on the façades, around the entrances and on the gables. Given our interest, we should be most attracted by Art Nouveau houses no. 612/23 from 1912 and no. 575/21, in the style of the late Art Nouveau, illustrated by their flat façades and geometrical decorations, wavy lines and striking oval-shaped golden tiles. House no. 612/23 has a beautiful original door ornamented with fine square pearl tiles in the interior. We will certainly notice two huge reliefs on the gable of house no. 575/21, dating from 1910. There are typical corner houses on both corners of Kodaňská and Norská Streets, their corners accentuated by towers. Two sculptures guard the entrance to house no. 33, built in historicising style - a bust of Vítězslav Hálek and a girl with a lyre - and a sign "Vítězslava Hálka, pěvce Večerních písní" (Vítězslav Hálek - the Bard of Evening Songs). An interesting feature is an opening above the door containing a coloured glass mosaic. Undoubtedly we shall also be impressed by the Art Nouveau grating. The opposite corner house has stunning relief stucco decoration in longitudinal bands with foliage and clusters of fruit, and outstanding oval-shaped tiles. Another remarkable house in Kodaňská is no. 61/43-45, built between 1911 and 1912 on a design by Antonín Bellada. The asymmetrical front is segmented by the various textures of the surface and enhanced by bay windows and balconies, which are prism-shaped and convexly arched.

Seemingly grey and plain houses with Gothic-style façades in Norská Street conceal inside their entrance halls superb stucco decoration, usually in Art Nouveau style, combined with fascinating patterns of ceramic tiling. Even whole pictures of landscapes have been combined in this way, such as in house no. 571/5.

We hope that this somewhat long walk around a formerly outlying district of Prague has shown the reader the variety of forms which Art Nouveau has taken in architecture. Its free ornamentation has been manifested even here, in blocks of flats built to serve this purpose.

14 WALKS THROUGH ART NOUVEAU PRAGUE

The ceramic Art Nouveau ornamentation around an unusual fountain in front of the children's home in the Krč district of Prague

Our walks through Art Nouveau Prague would not be complete without a look at the outskirts of the city. The walk will, however, take a slightly different form than that of the others. First of all take the bus from Vltavská station (on the C-line of the underground system) to Bohnice, a Prague district consisting mostly of modern blocks of flats. On the way we shall be able to see the Troja chateau and think over whether we shall have enough period to visit the famous Prague Zoo. But our main interest is the complex of the Bohnice psychiatric hospital. The whole complex has been set into a pleasant and quiet green park environment. The design of this complex, for that period definitely innovative for a hospital and garden area, was created by architects Václav Roštlapil and Václav Heller, and construction took place during the years 1904-1914.

The architecture of the main building, built in 1909, corresponds to the era of purpose-made Art Nouveau, and the frontal decoration respects the aim for which the building was erected. A plain white plastered front is divided up by ground and upper-floor window ledges. In the axis above the entrance, in an oblong niche above the window, we see statues of infant figures sitting on laurel wreaths and a symbolic snake, with a plate between them. The most striking decoration is the ceramic mosaic colour scene on the front gable which represents the healing of the sick and the inscription "AEDICATUM A. D. MCMIX". The building's overall style is Neoclassicist, though the façade bears the inevitable Art Nouveau decoration, repeated on the plaster of the neighbouring buildings.

In the interior of the main building we see that the entrance hall, corridor walls and staircases are lined with marble and that the hall has preserved its original mosaic paving. A two-branch marble staircase leads to the second floor, with a vast corridor supported by pillars. The most beautiful and most characteristically Art Nouveau elements are the brass banisters containing hanging wreaths of painted metal. Through a pretty door with a coloured glass mosaic we move from the basement hall to the main area of the hospital.

We are now offered a surprising view: the remarkably narrow and tall façade of the Art Nouveau church of St. Wenceslas rises a few metres farther away on a small hill. The tower in particular, with a battlement culminating in a cupola, towers above other parts of the church. It is worth inspecting the building closely. The entrance portal with reliefs is a copy of early Neo-Baroque style; however, the decoration is, in fact, Art Nouveau.

On both sides of the entrance we see statues of saints. An austere, flat frontal area is decorated only in the middle section by two colour mosaic scenes depicting the lives of SS Wenceslas and Ludmila. Mosaic pictures on religious themes can be found on all the church walls. The clock tower with a ceramic plate on the dial tells the time in all important places. Sculptured vases decorate the corner of the tower gallery. The northern orientation of the altar is an unusual feature of this church.

The sanatorium buildings, consisting of 32 pavilions, are scattered over a vast green area, which gives the patients a kind of privacy. Tidy roads lead us not only to individual pavilions, many of which have very modest Art Nouveau decoration, but also to a theatre. It has a very apt name, "Over the Fence", and has been architectonically adapted to the older buildings, although it was built later. The area is freely accessible to the public in the after-

The Church of St. Wenceslas in the grounds of the sanatorium in the Bohnice district of Prague is an example of late Art Nouveau work

The front gable of the main sanatorium building in the Bohnice district of Prague, an Art Nouveau structure from 1909

noons, and therefore we recommend that you visit this purpose-made building.

People living in Prague used to go to the other end of Prague, Krč, for Sunday outings to relax in the countryside, see the surroundings of the chateau and possibly stop at a restaurant. Today Krč is, naturally, a modern part of the town. In spite of that, in some streets Krč has maintained the image of a modern suburb with the great advantage of being near Krč forest. The journey, which used to ential a day trip, now takes a few minutes on the C-line of the underground system to Kačerov station, and then one stop by bus.

Along the street U Krčského nádraží in Dolní (Lower) Krč, around the former Art Nouveau Sun Hotel at no. 79/36, we reach a quiet area of villas and family houses located away from the urban sprawl. It is part of garden town planned at the beginning of the century in the suburban districts of Krč and Braník, the design having been masterminded by Prague landowner Tomáš Welz, and technically drawn up by the architect Bohumil Černý. Even at that time they emphasized the symbiosis of urban life and nature, an intimate environment, quiet in comparison with the hustle and bustle of the industrial town, a comfortable lifestyle from the point of view of finance and distance, and of course the artistic and craft work during the creation of a new residential area. Although this intention has not been fulfilled completely, a part of the project was realized here in Dolní Krč, near Krč railway station. In approximately 1910-1911 construction work began here, in the present-day streets U Kola, Nad Havlem, U Krčského nádraží, Paprsková and others. Some of these villas have been preserved nearly in their original form, and other, later reconstruction work has not hidden the characteristic features of the buildings. It can be seen that they correspond to the building work of the beginning of the century - a type of Art Nouveau villa - from both the architectonic and decorative points of view. All the buildings can be assessed as a complex of little villas, where their authors strived to do more than build a place to live in. A very interesting example is villa no. 151/8 from 1911 in Nad Havlem, a building employing late Art Nouveau decorative style, as can be seen on the rather flat front with a geometric plaster division, where blue oval ceramic decorations are an enlivening element. Below the main ledge we can see short strips with the prevailing vertical and horizontal lines, tempering the austere lines of the building. The builders succeeded in matching architecturally the garden and its fence. The opposite villa, no. 153/10, created by the same architect (probably Tichý), apparently has the same architectonic shape and decorations, including oval elements. Below the main ledge we find a band of rough plaster, ending in a wavy line which divides the plain plaster part of the frontal. A door between short brick pilasters leads to a slightly convex brick balcony. A prominent main ledge creates a sort of a huge niche for the upper floor windows.

A few metres lower down, at Nad Havlem no. 157/3, we see an interesting garden villa, "Ada", named after the wife of its first owner, Anežka. The villa was built in around 1912 by architect Beneš Pešina in an extremely short time: construction began in April, and by August the owners had moved in. The villa has a typical front gable decorated with wood and a combination of rough and smooth plaster; the balcony also contains wooden elements. The band below the main ledge consists of tiny geometric shapes filled with rough plaster and enhanced with oval ceramic tiles. Narrow windows leading to the garden still have their original bars. Paintings on the wall on the left of the entrance represent the Mother of God; they were executed by the original owner, Karel Svoboda. The Art Nouveau villa also includes a garden supplied by the Birka company together with the house. The delivery note includes planted perrenials, for example acacias, rowan trees, elms and silver spruce trees.

This district houses other remarkable villas, for example at Nad Havlem no. 179/4, at U Nádraží 164/26, and villa Roma at no. 148/28 from 1910. The design used a construction composition with a front tower and a protruding hall entrance, which is surprising for a small building, though it does not affect the pleasant impression it gives.

The visitor interested in the place where the famous Czech writers Antal Stašek, Ivan Olbracht and Helena Malířová lived, should turn into the street named U Kola to house no. 173/4, almost totally hidden in greenery. The house was built in 1905 by the Jan Řehák company and has now been reconstructed, but its functional composition has been preserved, as have the Art Nouveau elements: interesting bars on the terrace on the left, and a fragment of stucco vegetal decoration with the name of the villa, "Kamila", written in typically Art Nouveau style.

This part of Krč also contains other attractive family houses from the beginning of the construction work here, as well as from the 1920s. We should definitely not miss house no. 313/11 in Paprsková Street because of its bright combination of plaster on the front part of the building, and unplastered brick walls.

The idea of Krč as a recreational area with a healthy environment was confirmed in 1893 by the construction of a villa and pavilions on the edge of the Krč forest for the Emil Pavikovský spa. As a supplement a wooden decorative colonnade and pool were built. The whole complex of buildings was taken over by Dr. Šimsa, who bought it together with other land belonging to Tomáš Welz and, at the edge of a little forest in Dolní Krč, in Podlesí (as it is now known), he founded a sanatorium for the mentally ill. In 1910 the main building was erected on the basis of a design by the architect Bohumil Černý. Thus a complex area of villas called Rozkoš (decorated with an Art Nouveau wreath), Radost, Naďa, Inka and Orient was built. The main building, resembling a picturesque chateau, was called "Vita nova". And we should not forget the interesting Art Nouveau porter's lodge.

The mass of the building resembles the Baroque to a certain extent, in terms of its style, axis composition, volume gradation, and roof shapes, but the decoration betrays the influence of fashionable Art Nouveau ornaments. The larger and higher central part of the building gives the façade its imposing appearance. On the corners of the buildings we see slightly convex round bays. Along the whole length of the front, on the second floor,

An Art Nouveau brass banister on a staircase in the main sanatorium building, containing typically Art Nouveau wreath forms

The Neo-Baroque-style Art Nouveau building known as "Vita nova" from 1910, designed by architect Bohumil Černý, is situated in the Krč district of Prague

is a balcony with several doors with oval upper parts, a motif repeated in the interior of the building. The whole balcony is supported by columns which emphasize the articulation of the front even further. Along the building a covered arcade was created in this way. On the façade decorative Art Nouveau elements of wavy lines, ribbons enriched with glazed tiles and vegetal stucco ornaments appear. These decorative motifs recur also in the modest interior decoration, for example on the staircase banister and in the entrance hall on the column heads, panelled lower down with marble. The interior layout of the treatment and technical operation rooms is interesting.

The porter's lodge and the entrance were designed in a similar fashion to the main building, while in the case of many structures below the forest, their older origin in observed in the quieter, Neoclassical mass, Neo-Renaissance sculpted bossing or wooden festoons under the ledge. In 1920 the Czechoslovak Association for the Protection of Mother and Child in Prague 7 acquired the sanatorium with the help of the Ministry of Health, and from 1922 it served as a hospital and a place of refuge for mothers and children in Prague. It has the same mission at present, operating as a nursery home with a children's asylum at the Thomayer hospital in Prague 4. The institute is currently the only home in Prague able at any time to accept a small child in need of this type of care. It has a capacity of 140 children and 11 nurses, providing therapeutic, educational, rehabilitative and social-legal care for children and, if need be, for mothers as well. The work of the team of doctors, nurses and other workers is invaluable to society. Fifty per cent of the children have severe mental or physical handicaps. In spite of that the home must rely upon various charitable foundations for financial support to keep the hospital functioning.

Our walk ends with a visit to the lovely Art Nouveau building, the hotel Vila Voyta (formerly the Daliborka pub) in the K Novému dvoru Street at Lhotka. From the Nursery Home in Sulická Street we walk up to the Zálesí Street, through which we turn right and after a few minutes turn left into K Novému dvoru. On the corner we notice an articulated white and green building with a front turret and a wide covered entrance. The whole corner façade is a very interesting architectonic element, considering the plasticity created by the two equally high frontal gables on the side wings of the building. A ledge along the whole building, the narrow pyramid roof of the turret and the double attic windows on both sides of the building, are characteristic features. The façade is divided as far as the first floor ledge by bossing, and on the gables and in the horizontal bands between the windows it is decorated with white stucco ornaments. The overall architectural layout, the frontal, hotel interiors and garden, are an example of a purpose built Art Nouveau structure of this type.

The former roadside inn, built for Josef Vojtěch in Art Nouveau style in 1912, was purchased in 1990 in a dilapidated state and during 1991 underwent comprehensive reconstruction so that the Art Nouveau style and architectural expression of the interiors and exteriors could be renewed and the hotel could meet the standards of demanding customers at the same time. The complicated reconstruction and restoration in Art Nouveau style was professionally and excellently carried out by the architects Eva Heyworthová and Michal Postránecký. Visitors to the hotel and garden will be enchanted by the harmony of the colours, shapes, and materials used, and by the functional nature of the hotel. The door panels with figural and floral ornaments etched in glass, the harmony of metal and glass in the lights, and the artistic standards of the restaurant and hotel premises, are first class, and create altogether a stylish period atmosphere, with perfect service for the hotel guests, of course.

We hope that in escorting you on these walks we have fulfilled our promised aim: not only that of seeing Art Nouveau buildings and enjoying the work of Art Nouveau artists and craftsmen, but also that of taking a break from the busy town in the pleasant environment of the leafy suburbs of Prague.

The charming Art Nouveau Hotel Villa Voyta in the Lhotka area of Prague has undergone successful reconstruction

15 WALKS THROUGH ART NOUVEAU PRAGUE

The symbolic Art Nouveau mask of a girl on the façade of the Main Railway Station (Hlavní nádraží), an example of beautiful stucco artistic work and craftsmanship

Let us now begin a walk which will best illustrate the efforts of Art Nouveau architects, builders and artists to create buildings which meet the demands of the modern era and are of use to society and to the public: functional, and yet beautiful as well.

At the lower end of Wenceslas Square we turn right at the Koruna Palace into the street called Na Příkopě. Just on the left, opposite the Koruna, we see palace no. 1, at present the Commercial Bank building, built in 1908 by architect Josef Zasche, an austere modernist building, decorated only on the portals and the attic gable with bronze statues. The austere nature of the building contrasts with the decorative nature of the next house, no. 391/7. Here we have found one of the most famous Art Nouveau houses, which bears the gilded inscriptions U Dörflerů and Built 1905 A. D. on an ornate front gable. Generally the house

An oriel window of Hotel Central in Hybernská Street (no. 1001/10). Dating from 1900, it was one of the first Art Nouveau structures to be erected in Prague

is known as the Pelikán House, and a famous restaurant of the same name is situated there. The symmetrical house, with a slightly convex round bay on the front axis on the second to fourth floors, ends in a gable and a niche in which a large gilded vase shines. The plain frontispiece is embellished by green stucco decoration. The outstanding features are the wreaths and branches with ribbons. The windows on the third floor are guarded by stylized stucco pelicans holding gilded wreaths with a ribbon. Vases in other styles recur above the balcony banister with metal bars. The flatness of the upper part of the façade is interrupted by a protruding ledge decorated with tiny gilded consoles. The impressive nature and richness of the frontal are achieved especially through the rich gilding and soft green stucco on pale plaster.

At the late Neoclassical Church of the Holy Cross (built 1819-1823) we turn to the right into Panská Street, at the end of which, on the corner with Jindřišská Street, the renovated Hotel Palace, dating back to the year 1906, is situated. Built in Art Nouveau style, it is one of the hotels with the longest tradition in Prague. It is connected with the names of notable Czech artists, and has become a by-word for hotel comfort of an extraordinary standard. Hotel Palace offers guests a unique symbiosis of past tradition and luxurious modern comfort, plus an excellent location just a few dozen metres from Wenceslas Square and underground stations, and five minutes' walk from the Main and Masaryk Railway Stations.

Walking along Jindřišská Street, before reaching tall, late Gothic belfry, we turn to the left into the narrow and ancient Nekázanka Street. The prominent features here are the two bridge tunnels connecting important buildings from the turn of the century, built on designs by architect Osvald Polívka. The older building on the right dates back to 1894-1896, and was built for the Provincial Bank of the Czech Monarchy (now Živnostenská Bank) in Czech Neo-Renaissance style. The attic gable is strictly Neo-Renaissance; however, on the façade we find Art Nouveau decorative elements. A high three-storey frontal divided by stone ashlars culminates in a lunette with an allegorical mosaic of the history of the Czech nation, enriched by numerous

The gable on the house called U Dörflerů at no. 391/7 Na Příkopě, constructed in 1905 by builder Matěj Blecha, with its gilded sculpture of a vase in the niche

A mascaron on a residential building at no. 1984/10 Senovážné Square. Celda Klouček worked on the ornamentation of the building

The Jubilee Synagogue on Jeruzalémská Street, built in "Moorish Art Nouveau" style by Vilém Stiassny in 1906

fairy tale motifs reworked in sketches by Bohumír Roubalík and Vojtěch Bartoněk from sketches by Mikoláš Aleš for the Neuhauser company, which created the mosaic. On the mezzanine columns we see the allegorical reliefs Technology, Agriculture, Industry and Commerce by the painter Stanislav Sucharda and professor Celda Klouček, who is also the author of other decorative elements on the building's façade. Above the main ledge rises an attic floor. The busts on the attic were created by František Procházka and Antonín Folkmann. The allegorical groups on the corner of the attic gable were made by sculptor Stanislav Sucharda. However, this is not the end of the attic decoration, because between the vertical elements decorative mosaic fields with floral motifs made according to sketches by Anna Suchardová are located. The style and soft colours are a presage of Art Nouveau. In the bank's hall we find remarkable wall paintings representing St. Wenceslas and symbols of labour by Max Švabinský from 1896. Bronze statues of knights and torch-bearers, cast according to models by Bohuslav Schnirch, stand at the foot of the staircase. The staircase itself is decorated with paintings by Karel Vítězslav Mašek and Karel Ladislav Klusáček. In the hall, under a glazed ceiling, we can see allegorical figures symbolizing the Czech lands, by František Hergesel, Antonín Procházka, Stanislav Sucharda and Bohuslav Schnirch, and a fountain with figural decoration created by Ladislav Šaloun. The interior of the bank in particular makes a clear Neo-Renaissance impression and points to the wealth of the Prague burghers of the period.

During the years 1909-1911 a second Provincial Bank building was built on the opposite corner. The architect drew upon the main principles of the Czech Neo-Renaissance in Art Nouveau style, whilst the Art Nouveau impression is made by the front mosaic in three relatively individual fields, created on the basis of sketches by Jan Preisler. The mosaic lightens and articulates the whole façade. The sculpted allegories on the building's attic gable were made by Ladislav Šaloun and František Hergesel. Typical Art Nouveau decoration is employed only on the covered bridge tunnel closer to Na Příkopě. A ceramic mosaic relief with figures and a stylized tree stands out on its arch, and the upper part ends with a metal railing with floral ornaments in bars and with bases. At the foot of the arches of the bridge tunnels we can spot allegorical Art Nouveau masks. Visitors who would like to see one of the principal Art Nouveau architects, Osvald Polívka, are recommended to look at the bridge tunnel from the opposite side - the author of the bank's design looks down from the wall. Both buildings serve as an example of the gradual combination of Art Nouveau with former historicizing styles.

We now proceed along Na Příkopě past the Powder Gate and Municipal House, and turn into Hybernská Street. Approximately in the middle of the street on the right-hand side we find a charming Art Nouveau building, one of the first in Prague. Hotel Central was built on a design by architect Bedřich Ohmann in cooperation with Bedřich Bendelmaer and Alois Dryák, his pupils, in 1898-1900. On the flat façade with a slightly convex bay finished with a decorative little roof, the graphic floral ornamental inscription is very prominent. On the clear area of the frontal the large gold-coloured inscription Central is situated, underlaid by a red marble band and modestly situated symbolic branches with fruit, made more effective by their gilding. The whole front is enhanced by a combination of rough and smooth plaster and marble bands. The original look and form of the interior were changed by partial reconstruction and alterations in the early 1920s; for dozens of years the building served as a Chamber Theatre and became gradually run down. It has now been reconstructed and the new façade is striking.

At the first crossing beyond the Hotel Central we turn right into Dlážděná Street and arrive in Senovážné Square, where three Art Nouveau tenement houses with recently reconstructed façades (nos. 1984/10, 1985/11 and 1986/12) are worth seeing. The houses were built by architects Josef Podhajský and Matěj Blecha, and the stucco decoration was created by Celda Klouček; therefore, the frontals bear similar elements of Art Nouveau decoration, though each has its own personality. On the first three-axial house, no. 1984/10, we can admire the vegetal and figural stucco ornaments above the upper windows, on the side windows and around the entrance, with a beautiful mask and inscription "Anno domini 1903". The side gables over the attic are broken by round openings decorated with half-wreaths. The decorativeness and plasticity of the front of the house is achieved through rich stucco decoration, crafted balcony bars and a main ledge on consoles extending slightly over the middle part of the frontal in the same way as the higher triple gables above the side axes of the façade. In the passageway of the tenement house the original entrance staircase with marble banister and stucco decorations on the vault have been preserved. The view upwards from the staircase is enchanting. The Art Nouveau spiral staircase climbs towards the heavens, the floors are supported by marble columns with heads decorated with floral ornaments, and the view is rounded off by a glazed roof.

This magnificent spiral staircase at no. 1984/10 on Senovážné Square, with its imaginative lattice work and decorated columns, extends upwards to meet a glass dome

Hotel Palace, standing on the corner of Jindřišská and Panská Streets.
The Art Nouveau structure, dating from 1906, has undergone
comprehensive reconstruction work

A bridge serving as a walkway connects two buildings at nos. 858 and 857 Na Příkopě, designed by architect Osvald Polívka in Neo-Renaissance style, which then melts into Art Nouveau

The vaults of the domed foyer at the Main Railway Station are adorned with paintings and statues, created in keeping with the modern concept of a purpose-built structure in the Art Nouveau period

A wonderful ceramic picture of a woman on a pillar in the restaurant at the Main Railway Station, the work of the Rako company from 1903-1904

This ornate decoration in the foyer on the Main Railway Station serves as an excellent example of the artistic work and craftsmanship of the Art Nouveau period

On the middle house, no. 1985/11, our attention is attracted by a lunette which points to the predominantly Neo--Renaissance nature of the house. However, the coloured vegetal ornaments below the ledge and the other decorations on the house façade are Art Nouveau in style, and include balcony bars, doors with coloured glass mosaics, entrance corridors with stucco masks and ornaments, and landing windows with beautifully etched abstract flower patterns in the glass. The whole frontal is embellished by side balconies, and the gable with a round window generously decorated with ornamental vegetal motifs and swans on both sides is particulary interesting.

The third house does not leaves anyone in no doubt as to its Art Nouveau nature. Above all we notice the white façade with a plastic stucco relief of Madonna and Child in the centre of the third floor.

From Senovážné Square we move towards the tower in Jindřišská Street, but immediately turn left into Jeruzalémská Street, from where we can see one of the towers of the Main Railway Station. Before we reach this famous and magnificent Art Nouveau purpose-made building, we notice the remarkable articulated front of building no. 1310/7, which conspiciously differs from the Jubilee Synagogue nearby. It was built in a combination of so-called Moorish and Art Nouveau styles in 1905-1906 by architect Vilém Stiassny as compensation for three synagogues (Nová, Cikánova and Velkodvorská) pulled down during clearance work in Prague at the end of the 19th century. Typical Art Nouveau elements on the frontal can be found in the supporting and window columns on the heads of the half-columns in the basement and in a wreath of leaves above the single and double windows. The style of the building is shown also by the characteristic three-axial composition of the house and the functional layout of the interior. The combination of Neo-Renaissance with Art Nouveau decoration is more clearly visible on the next house, no. 961/5, from the beginning of the century, the façade of which is decorated with floral ornaments, and the portal with laurel wreaths. The area between the second and third floors is enlivened by two reliefs and stylized hop branches and fruit on the sides of the building in vertical strips. On the first floor the front is divided by ashlars. If we look upwards we see an arched gable with a window above the main ledge and a sculpted Czech lion above the window in a shallow niche.

Crossing the park (Vrchlického sady) we are now standing beside the new foyer of the Main Railway Station, the end of our walk. At first we pass through a modern part of the station from the early 1970s, with contains an entrance to the underground. Around the station a feeder road passes. A close inspection of the old station hall finishes and rounds off our impression of the Art Nouveau style of public buildings.

The construction of a new railway station became a vital necessity at the end of the 19th century because of the substantially increased demands of the developing town and, more especially, of industry. The design and acceptance of a project for such large construction work aroused much excitement among businessmen and the people of Prague in general. Architect Josef Fanta won the tender for the best project in 1900, and his design was implemented between 1901 and 1909. The station complex combines a functional and operational section with a representative element. The railway track itself was covered by a two-nave glazed construction, which expressed the demands of the modern era on a railway junction. The organic bend in the station roof showed the Art Nouveau sense of dynamism and a feeling of the common quality of both human and non-human organisms. The station building is made more considerable by the addition of wings, thereby giving it its imposing image. Moreover, at the time of its construction it was the tallest and the largest building facing the historic town, separating it from the newly developing industrial suburbs and creating a dominant feature of early 20th-century Prague.

The central pavilion of the station is an example of Art Nouveau. It consists of an enclosed semi-circular central area with a high portal and a glazed semi-circular triumphal arch. On either side stand high pylon towers with statues by Stanislav Sucharda and Hanuš Folkmann. The shape of the towers changes from a prism into a cylinder crowned by huge symbolic glass globes. The sculptural decoration of the hall was created by František Kraumann, J. Pikart and Bedřich Šimonovský, and the paintings were executed by J. Fröhlich. Magnificently composed, ceramic stylized scenes, typically Art Nouveau, supplied by the Rako company in 1903-1905, should be mentioned; they are to be found in the left wing, in the station restaurant area. The symmetrically situated lower wings of the building with the passenger service area also house administrative and management buildings with towers bearing a clock and statues by Čeněk Vosmík.

Fanta's station reflected the layout of the kind of railway station building used in the Europe of the period, a good example of which was the Gare de l'Ouest in Paris.

Prague Main Station, in the centre of the city near Wenceslas Square (the C-line of the underground system). The station building dates from 1901-1909

The station was initially named after Emperor Franz Josef I. After the Czechoslovak Republic was founded the station was called Wilson station, and later acquired the name Main Station. The name of US president Wilson was restored as an honorary title, "President W. Wilson Station", in 1991, during a visit by the then US president George Bush. The representativeness and luxury of the Main Station emphasize its importance as the main rail junction in the Czech Republic.

Whilst working on the text of this book, in addition to using our own information and arriving at our own conclusions, we drew upon the findings of research undertaken by the following architects and historians:

Olga Ambrožová, Marie Benešová, František Brabec, Zdislav Buříval, Alois Čenský, Alois Doležal, Oldřich Dostál, Jan Fischer, Ondřej Fischer, Jaroslav Herout, Jana Horneková, Lenka Hornychová, Emanuel Hruška, Yvonne Janková, Jaroslav Jásek, Karel Kibic, Eva Konečná, Jarmila Líbalová, Zdeněk Lukeš, Ladislav Machoň, Anna Masaryková, Bohumír and Marcela Mrázovi, Jindřich Noll, Vladimír Novotný, Josef Pechar, Vladimír Petrovský, Miloš Pistorius, Emanuel Poche, Rudolf Pošva, Jaroslav Soukup, Jaroslava Staňková, Jana Stehlíková, František Xaver Šalda, František Šmejkal, Ivan Šperling, Jiří Štursa, Ludmila Vachtová, Svatopluk Voděra, Aleš Vošahlík, Zdeněk Wirth, Petr Wittlich

MARIE VITOCHOVÁ
JINDŘICH KEJŘ

JIŘÍ VŠETEČKA

Cover, binding and typographical layout by
VÁCLAV RYTINA

Translation into English by
DENIS RATH and
MARK PRESCOTT, BA

First publication, Prague 1995

Published by V RÁJI Publishing House
(V Ráji 229, Prague 9), 1995,
19th publication, 184 pages,
164 colour photographs
Editors-in-chief:
Marie Vitochová, Kateřina Vitochová and Jindřich Kejř
Printed by
Tiskárna Pardubice,
Smilova 487, Pardubice,
Czech Republic